A Nest on the Highest Branch

*Reflections on Human Success,
Prosperity and Happiness*

A Nest on the Highest Branch

Reflections on Human Success, Prosperity and Happiness

Julio Savi

Royal Falcon Books

© National Spiritual Assembly of the Bahá'ís of India

First Edition: October 2003
Reprint: 2005

ISBN: 81-7896-022-2

'Royal Falcon Books' is an imprint
of the Bahá'í Publishing Trust of India
F-3/6, Okhla Industrial Area, Phase-1
New Delhi-110020, India

Printed at : Shri Manglam Printers, New Delhi-20

...if the qualities partake of the dust, what lasting result can accrue? The ideal to strive for is that which is in the supreme horizon—that is eternal! The underground is for worms and moles. That which is a cause for joy is a nest on the highest branch.

'Abdu'l-Bahá

Contents

Introduction	1
The Materialistic Conception of the Nature of Reality	7
The foundations of materialism	7
The denial of transcendence	8
The material world as the center of all human interests	10
The secondary importance of reason	10
A mechanistic conception of the world	11
The preeminence of material values	12
Individualism, relativism, and skepticism	12
Pragmatism, utilitarianism, and hedonism	15
The new dogmas of the modern Western world	17
The many sides of the modern West	18
Western Concepts of Success, Prosperity and Happiness	22
Success	22
Prosperity	23
Happiness	24
Progress	25
Development	26
Modernity	28
A Spiritual Conception of the Nature of Reality	31
Four criteria of knowledge	32
Is there a creator God?	33
How were the universe and humankind born?	36
Human Beings: Spiritual Creatures	38
Qualities of the animals	38

Animal limitations	39
The threefold nature of human beings	40
Contradictions of human life	43

The Nature and the Role of Religions — 47
Human greatness and limitations — 47
The founders of universal religions or
   Manifestations of God — 50
The role of religions — 57

Two Different Conceptions of History — 58
Modern conceptions of history — 58
A spiritual conception of history — 59
How to read the facts of history — 64
The lesson of history — 65

A Spiritual Conception of Progress, Development and Modernism — 72
Human progress — 72
A new concept of development — 79
The concept of modernism — 80

A Spiritual Concept of Success — 85
Acquiring spiritual qualities — 86
A spiritual path — 90
Spiritual qualities — 91
Spiritual transformation: the challenge
   of the modern age — 94
The culmination of spiritual evolution — 94
The results of a wrong choice — 95
Chance, fortune or will of God? — 97
Spirituality and poverty — 99

A Spiritual Concept of Prosperity — 101
Spiritual prerequisites of prosperity — 103
Social conditions of prosperity — 112

A Spiritual Concept of Happiness — 118
It is permanent — 118

It is a human capacity	119
The requirements of spiritual happiness	120
Spiritual happiness and wealth	128
Spiritual happiness and society	128

A Conclusion   **129**

Notes & References   131

Bibliography   144

Introduction

In 1978 the American writer Guy Murchie (1908-1997) wrote:

> After some five billions years of slow development, Earth is germinating in this very twentieth century and to some extent... in the centuries immediately preceding and following it, when so many fundamental developments have happened, are happening and will be happening to her.[1]

He then listed some 'evidences'[2] of this germination, including the most important innovations of the nineteenth and twentieth centuries. On the threshold of the third millennium, despite all symptoms of recession and the impending dangers on the future of the planet, his words still deserve our attention. Some of those evidences will now be listed and a few observations will be added, in the light of the events which transpired in the quarter century since the publication of his book.

A first evidence of the germination of the earth is the great expansion of human knowledge which occurred in the last two centuries, intended as the full range of scientific, technological and educational advances that have accelerated the pace of change and the transformation of society. This implies an impressive development in the technological tools at the disposal of human beings and, as a consequence, in their possibilities of practical realization.

A second evidence is the completion of the exploration of the surface of the planet. This completion, together with the remarkable progress in the quality, quantity and speed of the means of transportation and communication, has shrunk the earth into a huge village, whose inhabitants can meet each other or communicate with one another with maximum ease and speed, even if they live at the antipodes.

A third evidence is the proliferation of computation and automation, and the consequent revolution in the employment of human resources in work organization. The most unrewarding and tiring tasks have been passed on to machines, while increasing numbers of human beings are left free to devote their energies to more creative activities. Scientific and technological researches and discoveries have thus been greatly favored.

A fourth evidence is the outstanding increase of the total wealth at the disposal of humankind. Despite the unequal distribution of this wealth, this increase has produced a new vision of poverty. Today no one is willing to consider this unpleasant and still omnipresent aspect of human organized life as an unavoidable consequence of living in a society—escape from which lies only in the world beyond. Most people believe today that a good governance of human affairs can diminish the weight of poverty, promote an increase of the total wealth at the disposal of people and prevent its unfair distribution, and they ask that this be done.

A fifth evidence is the spread of standardization of many important instruments of social life in a world that has turned into a global village. The standards of weights and measures that in the past used to be quite different among different peoples are now converging towards a global standard, to the advantage of all kinds of international exchanges. The need is deeply felt for an international auxiliary language, so that the language barrier may be destroyed and people may easily understand each other and yet preserve the great wealth of their various idioms, a precious cultural heritage of all humankind.

A sixth evidence is the widespread extension of education, which was made possible through the intervention of many international and national bodies—such as the World Bank and many branches of the United Nations system— and which was speeded up due to the recent marvelous progress in information technology. This development has implied a radical shift of consciousness and a true revolution in the way people regard themselves and one another, with far-reaching results for all humankind. We will give a few examples. Women were typically considered inferior to men everywhere, but today they are steadily advancing towards equality with their counterparts. The ancient religious traditions that for long had ruled over the consciences of the masses, in many parts of the world have lost their hegemonic position. Some of their irrational aspects, conflicting with science and promoting ignorance and prejudice, have been openly defied. Growing numbers of people are totally refuting them. Many, who are aware of the importance of religious faith in view of morality, ask for religious teachings to be revised in the light of reason and of a peaceful interfaith dialogue. Although the twentieth century has been obscured by the ideological, dictatorial experiments of Fascism and Communism, it has witnessed a constant rise of democracy, intended as the entire social, political, and cultural shift that has increasingly transferred power from the few to the many. The evidences of this rise are many: the end of various forms of authoritarian rule; the increasing preference for states to establish governments through free and fair elections; the commitment of governments to involve people in policy formulation; the increasing emphasis on transparency, accountability and openness in governmental decision making; the fact that "'Unity in freedom' has today... become a universal aspiration of the Earth's inhabitants;"[3] the proliferation of mass media, including the Internet, which allows for unprecedented access to and sharing of information; the rise of people's movements and civil society organizations around the world; the growing respect for and protection of human rights for all.

A seventh sign is the growing awareness of the interdependence of all peoples and nations of the world. The process of nation building almost complete, the idea of nation seems on the point of taking on a quite different meaning than in the past. Despite some nationalist outbursts in different parts of the world, most people now seem to believe that loyalty to the whole world should be fostered above any national loyalty and, in fact, this best serves the long-term prosperity of individual nations. Besides, the globalization process implies an increasing movement away from one of the most disunifying aspects of nationalism, the concept of separate national economies. The two bloody world wars that laid waste the bodies and consciences of millions of people in the first half of the twentieth century and the discovery and employment of highly destructive weapons have brought about a revision of the meaning and nature of war. Despite 35 wars being fought at the end of the twentieth century,[4] increasing numbers of people call for the abandonment of this barbarian method to solve international differences and suggest less destructive ways, more suitable to human nature, which—according to many—is basically rational. Therefore the need of a firm international covenant is deeply felt, so that all the peoples of the world may live in peace. The idea of a world government was conceived at the beginning of the twentieth century by an American President, Thomas Woodrow Wilson (1856-1924). This idea has produced its fruits, in the League of Nations (1919-1946) and in the Organization of the United Nations (24 October 1945). The UN, now over its fiftieth year, is the object of attention of all the peoples of the world and their governments, who want to reform it so that it may more effectively work for of peace and justice. In the meantime enterprises for international co-operation have flourished all over the world in such diverse fields as science, education, law, economy, culture, philanthropy. These enterprises are preparing people for a higher level of unity.

In the last few decades some of these evidences have been grouped under the term 'globalization,' defined by the British sociologist Anthony Giddens as 'the intensification of worldwide social relations which link distant localities in such a way that local happenings are shaped by events occurring many miles away and vice versa'[5] and described by the American political scientist Walter Truett Anderson as 'a new arena (or theater) in which all belief systems look around and become aware of all other belief systems, and in which people everywhere struggle in unprecedented ways to find out who and what they are.'[6] Among the most important aspects of globalization, the English economist John Huddleston mentions 'the continuing growth of international trade as a proportion to the total economy... continuing improvement and intensification of international communication... the continued rise in importance of multinational and international corporations with their own cultures and a position increasingly outside the control of national governments.'[7] All these developments may be added to the list of evidences of the germination of the earth mentioned by Murchie.

All these events have implied a further development that, although sometimes ignored or underrated, is becoming increasingly manifest on the world's stage: a growing awareness that the peoples of the world are members of one and the same human race[8] and that this membership makes each of them equally important and equally entitled to the benefits of human civilization at the same level as the others. This awareness can be better defined as a blossoming consciousness of the oneness of humankind. It seems destined to grow within the consciences, and promises to be the instrument of a new era of human civilization. In this era each newly born human being will come to be welcomed as 'a trust of the whole,' and therefore the peoples of the world will wish to organize themselves in such a way that this 'collective trusteeship'[9] may be effectively provided for by their various governments.

No unbiased and attentive observer will fail to see that the horizons of the world are not particularly bright at present. There are many clouds, much injustice, many conflicts, many incumbent dangers, particularly for the ecological balance of the planet, and much opposition caused by short-sightedness, heedlessness, and selfish interests, to the global changes of the economical, social and political structures, which reason wishes, the masses call for, and the present situation enjoins.

However, the evidences of the germination of the earth are so manifest and unequivocal that increasing numbers of people are convinced that the peoples of the world have the capacity to plan just now, together, in peace, with confidence, a better future. A future when success, prosperity and happiness will be within the reach of all human beings. A collective will and a deeper awareness of certain aspects of reality are required, so that some nefarious prevailing ideas may be radically revised, for the simple reason that they have proved to be disastrous. The ominous events that cast a pall over the beginning of the new century and the clash between West and East that a number of people see going on in the world confirm the urgency and inevitability of this act of collective will and of this revision.

The Materialistic Conception of the Nature of Reality

When we speak of human success, prosperity and happiness, our readers will likely think of the prevalent ideas in the contemporary Western world. These ideas are strongly influenced by the materialistic conception of the nature of reality that became well established in that world in the last two centuries, as an outcome of the positivistic philosophy founded by the French philosopher Auguste Comte (1798-1857), and resulted in the analytical and linguistic philosophies of the second half of the twentieth century. Although most of its assumptions have become obsolete in the light of later philosophical reflections and scientific discoveries, Positivistic thought has become 'a central guiding thread in modernity's reflexivity'[1] and the pivot of that 'system of thought [that] reigns today virtually unchallenged across the planet, under the nominal designation "Western civilization,"' a system of thought which, '[p]hilosophically and politically,... presents itself as a kind of liberal relativism; economically and socially, as capitalism.'[2] One cannot for certain say that all Westerners share all its ideas, but undoubtedly most of them more or less share, its general trends.

The foundations of materialism

A comprehensive study of the prevalent Western materialistic conception of the nature of reality has been carried out by the Russian sociologist Pitirim A. Sorokin (1889-1968). Although his study dates back to the 1940s, it remains up-to-date. Its logical line will be followed, and a few comments will be added.

Sorokin reminds us that according to the materialists, the main instruments of human knowledge are the sense organs: 'their testimony decides what is true and what is false; they become the supreme arbiters of the validity of any experience and proposition.'[3] This philosophical assumption has far-reaching consequences on several aspects of human thought and life.

The denial of transcendence

First of all, this assumption implies the denial of any reality or value transcending the senses. '"We are not captive of superstitions;"' are the words 'Abdu'l-Bahá (1844-1921)[4] ascribes in 1912 to his contemporary materialistic philosophers, '"we have implicit faith in the impressions of senses and know nothing beyond the realm of nature, which contains and covers everything."'[5] And moreover:

> Order and symmetry is due to nature and its forces... composition and decomposition which constitute life and existence are exigencies of nature... man himself is an exigency of nature... nature rules and governs creation; and... all existing things are captives of nature.[6]

Therefore, according to the materialists, there is no God. In the 1970s the French scientist Jacques Monod (1910-1976) writes with absolute certitude:

> Pure chance, absolutely free but blind, at the very root of the stupendous edifice of evolution: this central concept of modern biology is no longer one among other possible or even conceivable hypotheses. It is today the sole conceivable hypothesis, the only one that squares with observed and tested facts. And nothing warrants the supposition—or the hope—that on this score our position is likely ever to be revised.[7]

And Karen Armstrong, one of the foremost British commentators on religious affairs, remarks in 1993 that whereas in the nineteenth and early twentieth century atheism was 'attended by doubt, dread and, in some cases, agonizing conflicts,' today it 'seems to have... become an automatic response to the experience of living in a secularized society.'[8] Moreover, according to the materialists, there is no immortal soul. Human beings are aggregates of material elements, and when these elements become decomposed, they cease to exist. A fruit of a wholly casual material evolution, they are direct descendants of animals and belong to their realm. The Spanish philosopher Fernando Savater upholds this conception when he writes:

> Darwin has quite convincingly demonstrated that our species is nothing more than one among many in the mass of living beings, that no God has created us in his image and after his likeness, and that we come from casual mutations of a long genetic line of anthropoid mammalians.[9]

Human mind is the product of biochemical activities of the brain, and becomes decomposed with it. The Italian psychologist Paolo Legrenzi takes this idea for granted: 'Giving for sure that our "mind" is a part of nature, investigable through the scientific method, has been one of the greatest intellectual accomplishments of the last century.'[10] Human sentiments and ideas are strictly dependent on genetic assets and bodily conditions, strongly influenced by the social milieu and only marginally manageable through the exercise of will. Human beings are a part of nature, 'a mere accident in the context of a process which... [develops] independently of them.'[11] They are destined to a complete 'physical subservience to nature's laws,'[12] and thus to a more or less strict dependence on their instincts. Religions, whose importance materialists could not deny because of their impressive presence in the past as well as in the present, are considered 'as the product of human striving after the truth, as the outcome of certain climates of thought and conditions of society,' and 'the reality or even the possibility of a specific revelation of the Will of God to mankind through a human Mouthpiece' is sternly denied.[13] And therefore it is strongly recommended that 'all spiritual phenomena must be understood through the application of a scholarly apparatus devised to explore existence in a way that ignores the issues of God's continuous relationship with His creation and His intervention in human life and history.'[14]

The material world as the center of all human interests

If there are no spiritual worlds, all human interests are turned towards the material world and all 'the spiritual impulses that distinguish the rational soul' are completely leached out of 'human motivation— and even interest.'[15] Sorokin writes:

> All the cognitive aspirations are concentrated on the study of these sensory phenomena, in their materiality and observable relationships, and on the technological inventions that aim to serve our sensory needs. Knowledge becomes equivalent to the empirical knowledge represented by the natural sciences.[16]

The secondary importance of reason

If the senses are the supreme criterion of human knowledge, reason itself, albeit appreciated and praised by materialists, occupies a place of secondary importance. This statement may be considered paradoxical by a number of people, because most Westerners usually maintain that the rational faculty is the supreme guarantee and the most effective instrument available to human beings and that human beings do not need anything else for their personal and collective progress.

However, these professions of faith in human reason conflict with a fact. The main reason why many Westerners deny or ignore transcendent reality is that it defies sense perception. This is the real foundation of all their objections against the rational proof of the existence of God, of the existence and immortality of the soul produced by the upholders of the spiritual conception of the nature of reality and against the concept of divine revelation, which is the foundation of all religions. It is evident, therefore, that whoever upholds the materialistic conception of the nature of reality also upholds the primacy of sense perception over the rational capacity, without realizing the contradiction of a conception which employs reason to deny the same instrument that formulates and justifies it.

The consequences of this ambiguity are manifold and very important. In essence, they imply for idealism to be excluded from whatever aspect of human life and for material reality to become the focus of general attention. Sorokin observes:

> A quasi-pornographic conception of human culture acquires a wide vogue, in biographies, history, anthropology, sociology and psychology. Anything spiritual, supersensory or idealistic is ridiculed, being replaced by the most degrading and debasing interpretations.[17]

A mechanistic conception of the world

If all is material, if even intellectual activities are a by-product of material phenomena, the unavoidable consequence is a 'general tendency... to regard the world—even man, his culture and consciousness itself—materialistically, mechanistically, behaviouristically.'[18] 'Abdu'l-Bahá remarked in 1912 regarding 'narrow-minded materialists':[19]

> The basis of all their conclusions is that the acquisition of knowledge of phenomena is according to a fixed, invariable law—a law mathematically exact in its operation through the senses... This, they say, is a fixed mathematical law of perception and deduction, the operation of which admits of no doubt whatever.[20]

Therefore materialists say that the universe was not created by a personal creator God, but by an unconscious power that operates within it. Most of them say moreover that the universe is a machine, wholly devoid of purpose and intelligence, functioning according to exact laws, as if it were a clock. In a way, therefore, the universe is predetermined by its own laws.

The preeminence of material values

A culture that is founded on such premises unavoidably emphasizes such material values as wealth, power, pleasures, and sex. Giddens observes: 'secularisation has the effect of narrowing down moral meaning to the immediacy of sensation and perception.'[21]

The Italian sociologist Roberto Giammanco, who describes American society as 'the winning-post and, at the same time, a necessary step... an essential dimension of contemporary man,' wrote that 'the best an American, all that his imagination can crave' is 'escaping from daily reality, deliverance from an enslaving work, game as the only content of life, prestige, beauty, power, health, adventure, pleasure.'[22] He remarks moreover: 'Children are reared so that they may be life's darling: their instincts are their only law. Everything is presented as a game: learning, working, loving, marrying, relaxing, doing politics, purchasing, dying.' And he adds: 'material development... is perhaps the only incentive of individual life.'[23] Material possessions are considered so important that some go so far as seeing their own identity as dependent upon those possessions and thinking that this has always been the case. Giammanco writes: 'Are you astonished at this craving for shopping, and at these useless attempts at acquiring an identity through purchasing an expensive car, or just a car with a greater number of chromium-plated or flashy accessories? Well, they will answer, man has always been the same.'[24]

Individualism, relativism, and skepticism

If the only reality is material reality as perceived through the senses, two consequences are unavoidable. First, since material reality is always changing, nothing is lasting and permanent. Second, since sense perception is the only reliable information, each thing has a relative value in relation to its perceiving subject. The individual is thus the center of all things and the value of things, which is changing and relative in itself, becomes even more so, because it depends on an always changing personal judgment. But if nothing is fixed, or reliable, no worthy universal truth or value exists. This is the origin of individualism, relativism, and skepticism that are so common in the modern Western world.

As to individualism, the leading British historian Eric Hobsbawm writes:

> The world was now [in the 1960s] tacitly assumed to consist of several billion human beings defined by their pursuing of individual desire, including desires hitherto prohibited or frowned on, but now permitted—not because they had now become morally acceptable but because so many egos had them.[25]

And he adds: 'The cultural revolution of the later twentieth century can... best be understood as the triumph of the individual over society, or rather, the breaking of the threads which in the past had woven human beings into social textures.'[26] In those years, the historian remarks, the British premier Margaret Thatcher said: '"There is no society, only individuals."'[27] Anderson describes individualism as 'the drift of cultural change... in the direction of forcing everyone to be free, requiring everyone to create a personal identity and experience, however sparse the resources.' And he adds: 'The struggle to be someone is a global struggle.'[28] Matthew Weinberg, a journalist and a senior officer of the Bahá'í International Community,[29] synthesizes this modern individualistic attitude in three points: personal prerogative defines the structure of society; '[t]here is no moral bond with others unless individuals choose to concern themselves with the interests of the community; rights [are viewed] as being prior to and often unconnected to duties. The rights of an individual are often seen as rights that provide immunity from communal interests.'[30]

As to relativism, it implies the belief that there are no universal values and therefore good and evil are relative. The same thing may be good for an individual and bad for another.

In 1982 William B. Provine of New York's Cornell University writes that there are neither moral laws in itself, nor absolute principles guiding human society, that human beings are amazingly complex machines, and that freedom, intended in the classic connotation of the term, does not exist.[31] In the same vein Anderson sees 'in our lifetimes the collapse of the objectivist worldview that dominated the modern era, the worldview that gave people faith in the absolute and permanent rightness of certain beliefs and values,' and the diffusion of constructivism. This is a particular form of materialistic relativism, whereby 'what we call the "real world" is an ever changing social creation;' 'all truth... [is] human invention. Whatever is out there... remains for all time out there, and all our systems of thought are stories we tell ourselves about something that remains essentially unknowable.' And therefore it is much better for a person to chose 'to live within a belief system for the simple comfort it brings and not because he or she considers it the last word.'[32] And the French historian Georges Minois suggests 'a generalized relativism and skepticism' as a meeting point between atheists and believers, a 'fascinating solution for minds worn out by their long journey through the millenarian history of human thought in a vain search after truth.'[33]

As to skepticism, Giddens describes among the typical features of the end of the twentieth century the fact 'that we have discovered that nothing can be known with any certainty, since all pre-existing "foundations" of epistemology have been shown to be unreliable.' And he explains: 'Although its originators [of modernity] looked for certainties to replace preestablished dogmas, modernity effectively involves the institutionalisation of doubt.'[34] But the person who believes in nothing may believe in anything.[35] And thus Anderson remarks that at the end of the twentieth century 'beneath the rational surface of the more-or-less secular "realism" that is supposed to be our official worldview... lurks a seething cauldron of cults and faiths of all description.'[36] No wonder that Minois writes that 'history will record the twentieth century as the century of the wreck of all certitudes... A crepuscular atmosphere which in a way gives the measure of the intellectual failure of a humanity that has come to despise reason itself.'³⁷

These assumptions have far-reaching consequences. The past is lost forever. The future is uncertain, and thus of slight importance. Only the present has a meaning and deserves our attention. Seize the day, everything and immediately. Only youth is acceptable, old age is a ghost to be exorcised and old people, its tangible and unwelcome proof, people to avoid. However, since '[t]o exalt such goals as acquisition and self-assertion as the purpose of life is to promote chiefly the animal side of human nature,'³⁸ egotistical passions prevail, unselfish feelings disappear, hearts grow callous, morals become loose. In 1999 the Bahá'í International Community wrote: 'The moral consequences [of the cult of individualism] have been corrosive for the individual and society alike—and devastating in terms of disease, drug addiction and other all-too-familiar blights of century's end.'³⁹ And thus, paradoxically, in the individualistic society where 'it is an imperative that every individual must accumulate ever more profit,'⁴⁰ processes 'that organize society so that it makes choices and takes decisions wherefor the individual is less and less important'⁴¹ prevail.

Pragmatism, utilitarianism, and hedonism

Sorokin observes:

> Since sensory cognition does not seek anything absolute… and since it views any 'truth' as a mere means of adaptation to the sensory universe, designed to make life pleasanter or less painful, the propositions and theories that prove to be useful, enjoyable and convenient become authentic, whereas those that prove to be useless, inconvenient, or non-economical are regarded as false.⁴²

This is the origin of pragmatism, formulated by the American philosopher William James (1842-1910), who thought that the 'only test of probable truth is what works best in the way of leading us, what fits every part of life best and combines with the collectivity of experience's demands, nothing being omitted.'[43] Therefore 'ideas and facts can be evaluated only from the point of view of their success, that is,... of their cash-value.'[44] This also is the origin of hedonism, that is, the quest for pleasure, with its corollary that each individual has 'the right and the freedom... to pursue happiness, unhampered by any commitment to society or responsibility for the suffering of others.'[45]

But the presence of pragmatism, utilitarianism and hedonism, reinforced by individualism and moral relativism, implies, as has been said, that interpersonal conflicts in view of achieving one's goals become more violent. Sorokin writes: 'Under such circumstances the struggle is bound to become ever sharper, more intensive and more diversified in its means and forms. The ultimate result is the emergence of rude force, assisted by fraud, as the supreme and sole arbiter of the conflicts.'[46] In 1995 the Bahá'í International Community wrote:

> Whether in the form of the adversarial structure of civil government, the advocacy principle informing most of civil law, a glorification of the struggle between classes and other social groups, or the competitive spirit dominating so much of modern life, conflict is accepted as the mainspring of human interaction.[47]

And in 1999 it wrote: 'Nurtured by such cultural forces as political ideology, academic elitism, and a consumer economy, the "pursuit of happiness" has given rise to an aggressive and almost boundless sense of personal entitlement.'[48] Thus the West has reached 'a condition approaching moral anarchy,' whereby most Westerners are ready 'to justify the most extreme forms of aberrant behaviour as primarily civil rights issues,' approve 'an almost universal celebration in the arts and media of degeneracy and violence,' explain the 'unbridled exploitation of the masses of humanity' defining the greed which is responsible for this exploitation as impersonal market forces, define the 'gross self-indulgence' that is responsible for 'the destruction of moral foundations vital to humanity's future' as freedom of speech.[49]

The new dogmas of the modern Western world

Most Westerners firmly believe that their materialistic conception of the nature of reality is logical and rational, and its conclusions are scientifically proved and irrefutable. A corollary of this conviction is the idea that whoever upholds the existence of a spiritual dimension of reality gives up using reason and puts his or her confidence on faith. But when materialists say that only the material universe is real and that, since the senses do not perceive any spiritual reality, this reality exists only in the imagination of those who conceive it, also their statement implies an act of faith, faith in sense perception. Moreover, since spiritual reality is by definition beyond the reach of the senses, whoever decides to rely on the senses as the supreme criterion of knowledge has no possibility of either demonstrating or denying its existence. Therefore also the materialistic conception is, in the words of Anderson, 'a belief, and in some ways an arbitrary one. It presumes, without knowing how to prove it, that there is an objective cosmos that we can seek to understand, even though all our understanding is always in a sense subjective.'[50]

Very often this faith which characterizes the materialistic conception of the nature of reality typical of Western civilization is strictly connected with faith in scientific and material progress. The journalist José Maria Sbert writes in this regard:

> Progress is a faith that is not recognized as such, but remains the genuine soul of the modern West and whatever comes to resemble it in the present world. Modern man has to believe that his ideas and actions are entirely grounded in what is rational and not supported by revelation, or a vision, or hope. His very identity has been forged in the conquests of progress, and centred on the conviction that he can know reality through science, thus overcoming obscurantist dogmas.[51]

Some scientists, who according to the materialists are the custodians of the highest knowledge, that is, science, began to understand long years ago that the foundations of materialism are unsound. In the 1930s the agnostic English philosopher Bertrand Russell (1972-1870) complained: 'It is a curious fact, just when the man in the street has begun to believe thoroughly in science, the man in the laboratory has begun to lose his faith.'[52] And he added in another context: 'In recent times, the bulk of eminent physicists and a number of eminent biologists have made pronouncements stating that recent advances in science have disproved the older materialism, and have tended to reestablish the truths of religion.'[53]

However, this faith in the materialistic conception of the nature of reality, mainly in its form as faith in science and material progress, is a preeminent feature of the prevailing Western mentality. It is often upheld with such strength that we may speak today of 'a kind of universal religion claiming absolute authority in both the personal and social life of humankind.'[54] This 'religion without God,'[55] 'claiming to be the voice of "science"' and seeking 'systematically to exclude from intellectual life all impulses arising from the spiritual level of human consciousness,'[56] is as dogmatic as the ancient religions which it sought to undermine. And its dogmatism, Weinberg observes, is 'just as pernicious as the religious orthodoxies that preceded it. Much of the confusion of contemporary life can be traced to the failure to tap in a balanced way the powers of both reason and faith.'[57]

The many sides of the modern West

No one can deny that Western civilization, characterized by this materialistic conception of the nature of reality, has produced certain advantages, mainly in its form of thought that is usually described as secularism and liberal humanism.

In the first place 'secularism played a pivotal role in freeing humanity from the shackles of religious fanaticism,'[58] which has been 'the greatest single obstacle against which the advancement of civilization has been forced to struggle.'[59] In the second place, secularism contributed to promote 'a culture which nurtured constitutional government, prized the rule of law and respect for the rights of all of society's members.'[60] And finally, it produced a model of life, the Western model, which most people consider excellent, because it is characterized by a high standard of life.

The reasons of the success of the materialistic conception of the nature of reality are many and quite complex, and their study goes beyond the intention of this book. However, this success has been assisted by a number of attitudes that characterized the old religions. They upheld the soundness of religious prejudices that promoted the discrimination of the followers of other religions and of the members of other races. And these prejudices have always produced terrible tragedies. They also upheld the soundness of 'fossilized religious dogmas that had lent moral endorsement to the forces of conflict and alienation.'[61] Most religious leaders of the time identified religion with an extreme defense of a past that many thoughtful people perceived as oppressive, and thus with an unmitigated struggle against modernity, even in its best aspects.[62] Disgusted by the prejudices and irrational dogmas taught by religions and by the intransigence of most religious leaders and allured by the most reasonable aspects of contemporary materialistic philosophies, many free thinkers refuted the dogmas and unacceptable customs altogether along with the noblest spiritual teachings of religions which called for moral discipline, moderation and wisdom. Another factor that contributed to the success of the materialistic conception of the nature of reality is the brutalization of human nature that, produced by the two world wars which darkened the twentieth century, has become 'an omnipresent feature of social life throughout much of the planet'[63] and has encouraged human beings to abandon a spiritual conception of life that was suggested by religions that could not avoid the horrors of those wars. Another factor have been the undeniable material advantages produced by science and technology, whose true voice materialism appears to be, and represented in the eyes of the world by 'the achievements of American capitalist culture.'[64] Last but not least, the upholders of theoretical materialism, which in the eyes of the world are the same as the upholders of Marxism, have seemingly defended the human rights, whereas religions—mostly 'driven back into fanaticism and unthinking rejection of progress,' or 'to a kind of personal preference, a predilection, a pursuit designed to satisfy spiritual and emotional needs of the individual,' and resigned 'to content... [themselves] with providing religious endorsement for campaigns of social change carried on by secular movements'[65]— seemed to defend them in theory but deny them in practice.

However, nowadays the advantages of the materialistic conception of the nature of reality and of the Western model of life which it inspired are surpassed by its damages. Secularism itself, having 'called into doubt both the spiritual nature of humankind and the authority of moral values themselves,'[66] is challenged by the many flaws that the materialistic conception has introduced into the behavior of those who adopted it and into the society they created. Many Westerners go so far as upholding that all human beings should be free to do whatever they wish and make them happy, so long as their actions do not harm anyone else. They also uphold that this freedom is more important than the observance of moral laws, most of which they consider as unjustified and unacceptable, since in their opinion they limit individual freedom and interfere with human self-realization. This idea that 'elevates acquisition and personal advancement to the status of major cultural values'[67] had far-reaching consequences. We will list only a few of them.

The first example is the crisis of the family. This crisis depends on many factors, including the changing roles of men and women in the new emerging society. But it also depends on other ideas. One of these ideas is that for both men and women, it is more important to follow the so called reasons of the heart, that is, one's passions, than observing the moral law of chastity, which is considered counterproductive. Another idea is that it is more important to pursue a misunderstood self-realization rather than observe the moral duty of loyalty towards one's partner, children, parents, brothers and sisters, which is considered as a limitation of one's personal freedom.

Another example is the widespread diffusion of rather

questionable patterns of behavior, inspired by 'the brutes in sports and movies, fraudulent profiteers in business and self-serving leaders in government,'[68] people who were successful in their lives, but at the cost of infringing on the spiritual principles of sincerity, loyalty, uprightness, generosity, etc. These two aspects of materialism have destructive consequences on society, one of whose cornerstones, the family, they weaken and on individuals, whose moral fiber they enervate.

A further example is the very poor condition of our planet, created as a consequence of an indiscriminate use of technology for personal and collective material goals without consideration to the spiritual principles of wisdom and moderation. Therefore it is not wise to consider the Western model as excellent since it allows high standards of living, for which an exorbitant price is paid. From the material point of view, it implies an enormous waste of energies and resources. It deprives the future generations of precious means, indispensable for their survival, it pollutes the world, and it concentrates wealth in the hands of a few individuals. From the spiritual point of view, it chases away any desire for spiritual elevation from the hearts of people. The psychologist Khalil A. Khavari remarks:

> Materialism is the religion of the age. It promises a false paradise—here and now on this earth, but delivers emptiness. It constricts our vision of what life is and what we are all about... materialism asks for no less than around the clock devotion to it. We drive ourselves hard, chasing after its spurious promises, but never quite capture them.[69]

But the most painful example is the 'damage done to generations of children taught to believe that violence, indecency, and selfishness are triumphs of personal liberty.'[70]

Western Concepts of Success, Prosperity and Happiness

Western concepts of success, prosperity and happiness are strongly influenced by the materialistic conception of the nature of reality described in the previous chapter, and are often connected with the concepts of progress, development and modernity. Whoever believes that human beings should be identified with their bodies and instincts, that material good is the only good, views success, prosperity and happiness as concerning mainly the achievement of material well-being, and conceives progress, development and modernity in terms of technological achievements. These concepts are clearly reflected by the various definitions of those words given by dictionaries and outstanding contemporary authors.

Success

The English word 'success,' originally employed to denote 'the degree or measure of attaining a desired end,' is now more commonly used to mean 'the attainment of wealth, position, esteem, favor, or eminence.'[1] The *Oxford English Dictionary* explains that 'success' means not only '[t]he fortune (good or bad) befalling anyone in a particular situation or affair,' but also 'the attainment of an object according to one's desire: now often with particular reference to the attainment of wealth or position.'[2] For a better explanation of this definition, the dictionary adds the following quotation by the American writer Oliver Wendell Holmes (1809-1894): '"Success" in its vulgar sense,—the gaining of money and position,—is not to be reached by following the rules of an instructor.'[3] The word success has similar connotations in other languages as well. In Italian, for example, the equivalent word *successo* originally meant simply 'favourable outcome, good result,'[4] but today it also has the more specific meaning of 'being in a sound economic position.'[5] According to William James, success is the proof of the validity of facts and ideas. It is highly significant that he refers to 'success' in this context through the locution 'practical cash-value.'[6]

No other definition given by dictionaries, no other statements written by eminent authors need to be quoted, to support the omnipresent idea in the minds of Western people that success has mainly to do with the achievement of economical well-being and the consequent power, 'understood as the capability of an individual... to exert its will over others.'[7] In these terms success is mistakenly viewed as the most important goal of life and the images of the ideal man or woman suggested by all kinds of media, and exploited by advertising agents, are based upon it.

Prosperity

The English word 'prosperity' means not only '[t]he condition of being successful, or thriving: a state of good fortune,' but also 'a state of high general economic activity marked by relatively full employment, an increasing use of resources, and a high level of investment.'[8] And the adjective 'prosperous' is defined as 'conducive to success... attended with or marked by good fortune... attended with or marked by economic well-being.'[9] In this dictionary no moral or spiritual aspects of prosperity are mentioned. The same is true for other languages. In Italian, for instance, the equivalent word *prosperità* is defined as 'enjoying affluence, economical well-being... a good standard of living characterized by good economic circumstances, health and high social prestige.' In the social and political perspective it is defined as '[a] condition of economic, political or social efflorescence of a state, a nation, a town, a society, a class, an industry; development and growth of an institution; a condition of power of an ideological group.'[10] Therefore also in the case of this word its material connotations are given prominence and its spiritual and moral aspects are ignored.

Happiness

The English word 'happiness' denotes 'the quality or condition of being happy... Good fortune or luck in life or in a particular affair; success, prosperity... The state of pleasurable content of mind, which results from success or the attainment of what is considered good.' And the adjective 'happy' is defined as 'having a feeling of great pleasure or content of mind, arising from satisfaction with one's circumstances or condition.'[11] The same connotations are present also in the equivalent words of other languages. In Italian, for example, the equivalent word *felicità* is intended both as 'a deep spiritual' and 'sensual enjoyment,' and in particular it also means 'prosperity, tranquillity, peace, affluence, well-being.'[12]

Although the terms 'happiness' and 'happy' do not imply in themselves specifically material or spiritual connotations, however, their popular meanings have been influenced by the present materialistic orientation of human minds. As it was quoted earlier, Giammanco wrote in 1964 that 'the best an American, all that his imagination can crave' is 'escaping from daily reality, deliverance from an enslaving work, game as the only content of life, prestige, beauty, power, health, adventure, pleasure.'[13]

The modern concept of happiness is also influenced by the typical individualism and relativism of the materialistic vision of life. Legrenzi remarks that 'American tradition... relates happiness to individual freedom.'[14] And the Italian philosopher Salvatore Natoli writes:

> Happy is whoever knows how to modulate the pace of life, how to find, each time, a measure among pain and joy... Whoever is happy... is always happy according to an idea... Therefore whenever happiness is mentioned, the different ways in which people feel happy are meant... Whoever believes in a transcendent world is waiting for a fulfillment, whoever is faithful to the present is looking here and now for the law of his satisfaction. Others will say other things.[15]

His words seem to suggest that human beings can be happy only with respect to the satisfaction of certain parameters of happiness which they themselves have decided, because there is no objective value on whose ground they could devise their strategies in view of its attainment. St. Augustine (354-430 AD) wrote quite different concepts: 'a man is considered unhappy when he is deprived of what he loves... But he is truly happy, not when he has what he loves, but when he loves what is worthy of his love.'[16]

Progress

Among the accepted meanings of the word 'progress,' in this context, we refer to 'the action or process of advancing or improving by marked stages or degrees: gradual betterment; especially: the progressive development or evolution of mankind... a theory that change from old to new is essential to progress.'[17] But the Western world has also ascribed to the word 'progress' conceptual connotations that the *Grande Dizionario della Lingua Italiana* [The Great Dictionary of the Italian Language] explains thus:

> Course, development of things and, in particular, of humankind, society and culture, according to a line of development which moves towards increasingly high, complex and perfect stages, with a gradual expansion of knowledge, ethical awareness, science, technology, social organization, and thus of well-being, freedom and, in brief, human happiness.[18]

In the course of the twentieth century, this concept of progress has gone through different stages, whose detailed examination would take too long. In brief, the idea of progress in the minds of people is now-a-days connected with a growth in scientific and technological knowledge and an improvement of the standard of living as a consequence of scientific discoveries, technological applications and industrialization. It also comprises a progressive emancipation of behaviors from the shackles of traditional morals, mainly in the sexual sphere, but also within the family, in all relations between children and parents, and in both the old and new generations.

The various ideas of progress have always implied hope in a steady and progressive improvement of life. As to the necessary instruments for this improvement, Sbert remarks that Westerners seemed to believe that 'the moral perfection of humans' could be achieved through 'the exhaustion of greed through the satiation of appetites, or... some prodigious balancing act of egotistical forces,' worked out 'by reason, but of a kind which had no known locus since it rested neither on God's providence, nor individual experience, nor revealed truth, nor moral tradition.'[19] Unfortunately this 'hope for the moral perfection of humans'[20] did not come true. Giammanco remarks that in the American society of the 1960s 'progress became the realization of conditions whereby the "fittest" could survive and flourish and, in the popular belief, the presence of human beings fitter for the struggle in view of acquiring and controlling wealth came to be considered as the only guarantee of progress.'[21] Evidently material progress, far from almost automatically implying a human moral improvement, heightens the spirit of competition, that is, one of the behaviors typical of the animal world, and favors the strongest, who is often the most shrewd and unscrupulous.

Development

The Mexican intellectual Gustavo Esteva writes: 'In common parlance, development describes a process through which the potentialities of an object or organism are released, until it reaches its natural, complete, full-fledged form.'[22] Then he examines the meanings that this word took on in the second half of the twentieth century, after Harry S. Truman (1884-1972), the American President, set forth in the inaugural address of the Congress he delivered on 20 January 1949 a concept of development as helping 'the free peoples of the world, through their own efforts, to produce more food, more clothing, more materials for housing and more mechanical power to lighten their burdens.'[23] Esteva also mentions a number of definitions of development, for example 'growth in the income per person in economically underdeveloped areas,' or development of 'the basic social services and the "caring professions" found in the advanced countries' in those areas where they are still absent.[24] These ideas are reflected in the meanings that the *Oxford English Dictionary* ascribes to the locution *developing country* and the *Webster's Third New International Dictionary* attaches to the adjective *underdeveloped*, which entered in everyday language since President Truman used it in his above mentioned speech. The locution *developing country* is defined as 'a poor or primitive country which is developing higher economic, industrial, and social conditions.'[25] And the adjective *underdeveloped* is explained as 'failing to realize a potential economic level of industrial production and standard of living because of lack of capital for exploitation of natural resources, shortage of technically trained personnel, low medical standards, or because of culture traits resistant to change.'[26]

These ideas of development had many supporters. Among them is the Italian journalist Piero Angela who writes:

> Technology... is the true source of economic and political change in our societies. If any society wants to have a better standard of living, hospital, schools, higher salaries, free time, a greater equality between individuals, more education, the emancipation of women, etc., we can easily understand that all these things are an almost automatic by-product of technological development, whatever the political or ideological model of that society may be.[27]

In this sense Wolfgang Sachs, the German exponent of the green movement, writes that development means for Westerners 'the Westernization of the world.'[28]

The Bahá'í International Community remarks, in a document published in 1995, that all plans for development that are being now formulated are based upon a materialistic concept 'defined in terms of the successful cultivation in all societies of those means for the achievement of material prosperity that have, through trial and error, already come to characterize certain regions of the world.' And it regrets that although Western society accepts the principle of participation, it imposes on the various peoples 'a range of choices formulated by agencies inaccessible to them and determined by goals that are often irreconcilable with their perceptions of reality.'[29]

In recent years, a deeply felt need of 'accommodating differences of culture and political system and responding to the alarming dangers posed by environmental degradation' has slightly changed the general trend. But the materialistic assumptions are far from being abandoned, as it would only be right to do, in view of the fact that 'for the vast majority of the world's population, the idea that human nature has a spiritual dimension—that its fundamental identity is spiritual—is a truth requiring no demonstration,' and after having ascertained not only 'the ever-widening abyss that separates the living standards of a small and relatively diminishing minority of the world's inhabitants from the poverty experienced by the vast majority of the globe's population,'[30] but also the 'damage to the physical environment of the planet on a scale so massive that it may take centuries to heal.'[31]

Modernity

The *Grande Dizionario* defines the Italian word *modernità*, the equivalent of the English 'modernity,' as:

> All the aspects and manifestations of the material, social, spiritual, and cultural life of technological progress and customs of modern times... A proclivity to adapt oneself to, or to comply with, the mentality, the exigencies, the taste, the feelings, the more advanced and progressive customs, the way of thinking and behaving in contemporary life, in both one's practical and intellectual activities, as well as to refuse certain aspects of the past, in search of originality or because of a spirit of independence.[32]

This complex definition of modernity first of all describes the identification between modernity and technological progress, a concept that is supported by great numbers of people who consider the development of technology as the most salient feature of modernity. It also emphasizes a faith in progress and the concept that whatever is modern is 'more advanced and progressive,' and therefore better than whatever was in the past. It then puts the accent on the consequent idea that past conceptions should be discarded, because they are obsolete and outworn. As Giddens says: 'Inherent in the idea of modernity is a contrast with tradition.'[33] And the French anthropologist Gérald Berthoud refers to modernity as a 'radical project to create a new man and a new society.'[34] Finally this definition explains the motivation of all those who want to introduce these innovations, that is, 'in search of originality or because of a spirit of independence.' Sbert remarks that 'faith in progress,' which he considers as the foremost aspect of modernity, 'is faith in a purely intellectual, mathematical, scientific knowledge, "liberated" of all moral constraint and ethical context.'[35]

***

It is very clear now-a-days that the majority of those who share the Western concepts of success, prosperity and happiness as well as of progress, development and modernity are destined to miss their goal. If success means achieving wealth and social position and failure means being deprived, in a given moment, of whatever the market offers and whose possession society considers a sign of success, successful people can be very few. The masses are destined for failure. And if happiness depends on that kind of success, those masses are destined to be unhappy. If progress, development and modernity mean the Westernization of the world, the achievement of this goal would imply such an ecological derangement that the planet could be destroyed. In any case, for the time being, the Westernization of the world is causing the masses of poor people to become even poorer. Sachs bitterly remarks: 'The idea of development stands like a ruin in the intellectual landscape. Delusion and disappointment, failures and crimes have been the steady companions of development and they tell a common story: it did not work.'[36]

We certainly do not want to support the ancient mistake of considering poverty and pain as unavoidable aspects of life, because they will disappear in the life beyond. We may agree with the notion 'connected with the [American] spirit of frontier' as explained by Legrenzi, that we should 'learn how not to be unhappy,' through learning 'how to be different, how to improve,' but we cannot agree with his recommendation 'to go closer to that standard of "happiness" which society acknowledges and rewards.' We think that it is much better today to keep at a safe distance from the assumptions of the materialistic conception of the nature of reality, and to try to discover a new vision that may enable us to preserve a healthy balance between the material and spiritual aspects of reality. Then perhaps we will better understand what we should do in order 'to create the conditions whereby [happiness] may be realized'[37] within ourselves as well as in the world outside.

A Spiritual Conception of the Nature of Reality

Beside the materialistic conception of the nature of reality there is the spiritual conception, which is rooted in the spiritual teachings of the universal religions,[1] for example Hinduism, Judaism, Buddhism, Christianity and Islam. Some of its fundamental assumptions will be expounded in the light of the teachings of the latest among them, the Bahá'í Faith.

The spiritual conception of the nature of reality is quite different from the materialistic one in its fundamental theoretical presuppositions and in most of its practical aspects. However a few possible misunderstandings must be immediately cleared up. In the first place, this conception is inspired by the spiritual teachings of religions, which are universal, and therefore cannot be identified with any of those modern types of religiosity which are usually called fundamentalism, and which, in the words of Armstrong, elevate 'the value of the tribe to an unacceptably high status... [substitute] man-made ideals for the transcendent reality which should challenge our prejudices... [and also deny] a crucial monotheistic theme... the ideal of compassion.'[2] Moreover, this spiritual conception appreciates reason and its use in view of solving the spiritual, intellectual and material problems of life. It does not exclude confidence in science and its methods and ascribes a great importance to the development and progress of all the peoples of the world. And yet, since it is founded on the assumption that material reality is part of a larger spiritual reality and that there is a reciprocal influence between the material and spiritual conditions of the world, that human beings are creatures born from the realm of nature, endowed with an intelligence and capable of evolving towards spiritual worlds, that 'the working of the material world is merely a reflection of spiritual conditions,' and therefore 'until the spiritual conditions can be changed there can be no lasting change for the better in material affairs,'[3] it suggests that sensory data and rational deduction should be complemented by the guidance of scriptural teachings and the light of intuition, that the applications of science and the employment of technological products should be controlled by universal, essential spiritual principles or values, and that the progress and development of people should be promoted while observing certain fundamental spiritual laws.

Four criteria of knowledge[4]

One of the assumptions of the spiritual conception of the nature of reality is that the human criteria of knowledge are not two, as the materialists uphold, but four: the senses, reason, insight and Scriptures. Each of these criteria is equally important, but also fallible and limited, since human beings themselves are limited. Even Scriptures, which according to the upholders of the spiritual conception contain fundamental verities that cannot be ignored, can be fallible as a criterion of knowledge. This is due to the fact that they are accessible to human beings through their rational faculty, and therefore they become fallible once they have been interpreted. The use of all these four criteria, with the exclusion of none of them, is indispensable in view of an objective knowledge. But this goal of objectivity also requires the observance of general spiritual principles of detachment, sincerity, intellectual honesty, humility, wisdom, determination, steadfastness, devotion, etc., in whose absence no human enterprise has any hope of success. It requires moreover the awareness that the human mind may easily fall a prey to prejudice, intended as 'an emotional negative generalization… a feeling, not easily changed by reason, fact or education.'[5] However, the guarantee of the soundness of our knowledge rests only in the proof of facts, which may deny or confirm it. In a moral context, the soundness of a decision is demonstrated only when its application in daily life bears results of personal and collective harmony and peace, justice and unity. This is a true scientific method. First, data are collected. Second, an hypothesis that may explain them is formulated through the four criteria of knowledge. Third, the hypothesis is verified in the proof of the facts, in the results of its application. This method does not warrant the discovery of absolute verities, which are anyhow precluded to human beings because of their inherent limitations. It makes us discover relative verities, which are very useful because of the fruits of harmony and peace, justice and unity, which ensue from their practical application in daily life. A reconciliation is here attained between two seemingly irreconcilable tendencies: on the one hand, the persuasion that there is an absolute Truth—and this may be found in Scriptures, and on the other the awareness that any human truth is relative, comprising our understanding of the 'infallible' Scriptures—and this awareness is a sound protection against any unhealthy fundamentalism.

This method of investigation of reality can confirm the existence of a spiritual dimension, although this dimension is not directly accessible to the senses. In fact we can identify, in the material world, a number of signs through which we can suppose its existence. Facts will confirm the soundness of our hypothesis, through the fruits of harmony and peace, justice and unity, which ensue from its practical application.

Each individual follows a different road in his or her identification and interpretation of the signs of reality. We will follow a logical thread, but we do not certainly pretend it to be the best or the only one possible.

Is there a creator God?

Most human beings search for an answer to this question: is there a creator God? Throughout history theist, pantheist and deist philosophers[6] suggested various so called rational proofs of the existence of God. Throughout history materialist philosophers have refuted all of them. Experience teaches that very few atheists have been convinced to believe in God by one of those proofs. Nay, at the end of the twentieth century, according to Minois, in the opinion of Western intellectuals 'God is no more the central issue. This issue fades into the background and no one is anxious to repropose any proof. God is either accepted, or denied.' And then he adds: 'atheism is the common and immediate position. It is almost taken for granted.'[7]

However, one of those proofs is so attractive that it deserves mention. In a letter written as an answer to the Swiss scientist Auguste-Henri Forel (1848-1931), an upholder of positivism, 'Abdu'l-Bahá worded it in the following way:

> Now, formation is of three kinds and of three kinds only: accidental, necessary and voluntary. The coming together of the various constituent elements of beings cannot be accidental, for unto every effect there must be a cause. It cannot be compulsory, for then the formation must be an inherent property of the constituent parts and the inherent property of a thing can in no way be dissociated from it, such as light that is the revealer of things, heat that causeth the expansion of elements and the solar rays which are the essential property of the sun. Thus under such circumstances the decomposition of any formation is impossible, for the inherent properties of a thing cannot be separated from it. The third formation remaineth and that is the voluntary one, that is, an unseen force described as the Ancient Power, causeth these elements to come together, every formation giving rise to a distinct being.[8]

Usually faith in God is the result of various reflections on some of the features of the material world, on many facts of its evolution, on human evolution and history, as well as on several feelings born from one's personal experience. And these reflections and feelings are quite different for various individuals. In this regard, a suggestive anecdote is related about Charles Boyle, Earl of Orrery, who lived in southern Ireland early in the eighteenth century.

A Spiritual Conception

Having heard of Kepler's famous discovery of the laws of planetary motion and of Newton's recent work on gravitation, Lord Orrery had a working model of the solar system built inside his castle. It was an extraordinary, dynamic and up-to-date piece of clockwork with orbital hoops and a brass sun in the center plus smaller globes representing Mercury, Venus, Earth, Mars, Jupiter and Saturn slowly revolving around it, even a moon circling the Earth and four little ones going around Jupiter.

But it seems that Lord Orrery had an atheist friend who had an utterly materialistic outlook and thought of the universe as just an immense moving system of natural machinery that somehow coasts along, blindly but automatically maintaining itself without benefit of consciousness, mind or intelligence of any kind. So when the friend heard of Orrery's new and wonderful machine, he lost no time in going to the castle to see it. Entering the great hall where the model was in operation, the atheist's eyes widened with awe and the first question he asked Lord Orrery was: 'Where did you get this magnificent thing? Who made it?'

But Orrery, remembering previous arguments with the atheist about creation, surprised him by replying, 'Nobody made it. It just happened.'

'How could that be?' retorted the atheist. 'Surely these intricate gears and wheels couldn't create themselves. Who made them?'

Lord Orrery stood his ground, insisting that his model of the solar system had just happened by itself. Meantime, the atheist worked himself into a state of hysterical frustration. Then at last, judging the time was ripe, Orrery let him have it. 'Up to now,' he declared, 'I was testing you. Now I am going to offer you a bargain. I will promise to tell you truly who made my little sun and planets down here as soon as you tell me truly Who made the infinitely bigger, more wonderful and more beautiful real sun and planets up there in the heavens.'

The atheist turned a little pale and, for the first time, began to wonder whether the Universe could really have made itself, or possibly be running all this time automatically and unguided by the slightest twinge of intelligence. And this was the origin of the Orrery Theorem which says: 'If the model of any natural system requires intelligence for its creation and its working, the real natural system requires at least as much intelligence for its own creation and working.'[9]

Having faith in God means having faith in an unknowable Essence, that has willingly and consciously created the material universe we directly come to know through the senses, as well as the spiritual worlds whose existence we may prove through our rational faculty, although our senses do not perceive them, and that constantly guides His creatures in their continuous movement towards a purpose known in its entirety only to Him and but partially comprehensible to them.

How were the universe and humankind born?

According to those who believe in God, the universe is not the fruit of chance, but of the loving and conscious will of a creator God. According to them, saying that the universe was formed by chance is the same as saying that if a hypothetical painter would take a number of tins filled with paint of different colors, and then randomly throw them against a wall, and repeat this action an *infinite* number of times, after an *infinite* number of attempts, a harmonious fresco could appear by chance on that wall instead of the usual hotchpotch of colors. According to those who believe in God, the universe is not a machinery predetermined by mathematical laws, as a clock. It is an organism, which grew and is growing according to a plan, guided by an unknowable Essence. That unknowable Essence progressively draws the universe towards Itself, organizing it in increasingly complex forms which enable it to manifest Its spiritual

A Spiritual Conception

qualities on the material level and with increasing perfection.

In fact the history of the universe as described by scientists has all the features of the growing process of an organism. From an initial unitary stage, similar to that of a fertilized ovum, it has gone through succeeding stages characterized by an increasingly complex organization of its composing elemental particles. This increasingly complex organization has enabled the universe to express increasingly complex capacities: initially, the power of attraction typical of the mineral world, then the power of growth typical of the vegetable world, then the power of sensory perception typical of the animal world, and at last the rational power typical of the human world.

The whole process of the growth of the universe, studied and described by scientists according to the criteria of the theory of evolution, is a process of production whose fruit is humankind. Human beings in fact have the capacity of expressing all the powers of the kingdoms below their kingdom. But they also have the capacity of expressing powers that do not exist in those kingdoms. These powers distinguish them from all other creatures and can be better described through a comparison between the human beings and the animals, the evolutionary stage immediately inferior to them.

Human Beings: Spiritual Creatures

Qualities of the animals

The foremost qualities which characterize animals in their more advanced forms are as follows:

1. Sense perception and the sense of feeling, which are very similar to those of human beings.

2. Memory. Animals have the capacity of preserving a trace of previous sensorial experiences. This capacity, sometimes even stronger in them than in human beings, is indispensable both for those genetically programmed behaviors we call instincts, and for the animals' better adaptation to the environment, in view of enhancing the possibilities of survival of the individual animal and of the conservation of the species.

3. Learning. Animals can be trained so that they learn how to live with human beings and how to perform simple works for them. Moreover, recent studies on animal behavior made by zoologists and ethologists, have proven that they can learn simple operations to achieve goals connected with their instincts, from their parents, other animals, and their environment, even without any help from human beings.

4. Voluntary movements. Due to their instincts and memory of previous sensorial experiences, animals can voluntarily move about with a view to the gratification of their instincts.

5. Natural emotions. Animals are genetically programmed for certain instinctive behaviors, which are attended by emotions like rage, fear, greed, etc. These emotions and behaviors are intended for the survival of the individuals and the preservation of the species.

They also comprise certain kinds of elemental attraction and selective affinities, which are very similar to that feeling which is usually called love—for instance, couple bonds, parental bonds, group solidarity, attachment to human trainers, and last but not least a number of altruistic behaviors as the sacrifice of life for the sake of the offspring or species survival.

Animal limitations

With all these capacities, animals seemingly possess a sort of abstract activity and reality, which might well be defined as mental. Nevertheless their primordial psychism is curtailed because of some important features:

1. Animals have no power of conscious reflection and abstract reasoning and therefore they are captives of the senses, their only cognitive instrument.

2. They do not possess any self-consciousness or any consciousness of their own body besides its sensations and instincts. The more carefully trained chimpanzee, in front of a mirror, does not recognize itself in the image reflected in the mirror.

3. They are deprived of the power of meditation.

4. They are utterly lacking in spiritual susceptibilities and incapable of understanding the divine teachings. They do not conceive either God, or the spiritual worlds, and therefore they do not know any religion or Scripture.

5. They do not have the capacity of establishing standards of values in relation to a supreme good, but they react instinctively to each situation according to the peremptory requirements of individual survival and the preservation of species, which are the supreme, unreflective good for them.

6. They have the liberty to gratify whatever their impulses and proclivities may be, and yet they are captives of nature, since they cannot deviate from the road that nature has established.

These limitations have far-reaching consequences upon the life and development of animals. On the one hand, their possibilities of progress are limited to the physical realms. They have been created for the life of this world. They are perfect when their body is healthy and their physical senses are whole. But this same, already accomplished, natural perfection is a great limitation as well. No animal species has created a civilization that has progressed century after century as human beings did. On the other, since animals are wholly unconscious of spiritual life, they are the embodiment of perfect liberty, that is, the gratification of their instincts. When their body is healthy and their physical senses are whole, they have attained the fullest degree of physical felicity. However, this same freedom is, in another respect, captivity: the servitude to natural laws. The struggle for existence with the physical survival of the fittest is the inexorable law of their lives. Therefore they are forever condemned to be subjected to their sensuality, unbridled instincts and passions, and their accompanying succession of sorrows, cruelty, oppressions, deception, tyranny, ruthlessness.

Therefore, the fundamental difference between human beings and animals, that *quid* whose presence enabled humankind to evolve throughout the ages and whose absence kept animals stationary in their natural sphere, is not where it has mostly been looked for up to now. Animals too possess a sense of feeling, a certain degree of intelligence and will, a certain capacity of invention, memory and a limited capacity of material progress, emotions and affinities. And all these qualities make the animals worthy of the greatest respect from human beings. However, it is not these qualities that we should investigate, to find a typically human *quid*.

The threefold nature of human beings

According to the spiritual conception of the nature of reality, we can distinguish in human beings a threefold nature: material or animal, human and spiritual.

The material or animal nature

The material or animal nature of human beings is the most obvious and manifest for all. It depends on the body and is manifest as the 'self,' which in this context may be defined as the consciousness of one's body and its instincts which each human being acquires and preserves during his or her earthly life. Instincts are certain physiological activities and particular behaviors required for certain physical goals to be achieved—preservation, reproduction and regulation. They are realized through biochemical and neurohormonal mechanisms, regulated by a sequence of chemical instructions contained in the genetic code. Instincts are perceived and manifest themselves as emotions, for example, the struggle for survival, fear, anger, desire, passion, greed, avarice, revenge, deception etc. In human beings these emotions are empowered through the use of the rational faculty and give rise to subtler, more complex and changeable behaviors than in the animals. 'Abdu'l-Bahá describes the material or animal nature of human beings as 'the insistent self, the evil promptings of the human heart.'[1] However, this nature is not to be considered 'evil' in itself. Undoubtedly it is not evil in the animal. But since human beings also have the capacity to express a superior nature—which their material or animal nature is inclined to ignore and to stifle—such a nature, relatively speaking, may be 'evil.'

The human nature

Human nature, that is, the rational faculty, is obvious, and even materialists recognize it. However, they identify it with biochemical activities of the human brain, different from equivalent activities of the animals only because of their greater complexity, whereas, according to the upholders of the spiritual conception, the rational faculty is a power of the human soul that becomes manifest through biochemical activities of the brain. It can be defined as 'the power by which man acquires his knowledge of the several kingdoms of creation, and of various stages of existence, as well as of much which is invisible,'[2] and it implies a thirst for knowledge that 'Abdu'l-

Bahá defines as 'love of reality.'[3] As has just been said, this faculty is absent in the animal world. When human beings turn their rational faculty towards the spiritual worlds, they develop an aspiration to rise towards those worlds, that are always perceived as better than the material one. This is the simplest expression of the spiritual nature of human beings.

The spiritual nature

The spiritual nature of human beings is denied by the materialists. And yet the Scriptures say that human beings were created at His image and after His likeness,[4] in the sense that God has bestowed upon them the capacity of mirroring forth all His divine attributes in the form of human virtues. This is the spiritual nature of human beings, an outer manifestation of that personal and immortal spiritual reality which is usually called soul. The soul may be described as the center where 'the perfections of God, the divine virtues, are reflected or revealed,'[5] or the 'inner... [and] conscious reality'[6] of human beings, the seat of their individuality. Therefore the Bahá'í writings describe human beings 'as a mine rich in gems of inestimable value.'[7]

Also of the existence and immortality of the soul, as of the existence of God, theistic and deistic philosophers have produced rational proofs, which materialist philosophers have regularly refuted. Also in this case faith in the existence and the immortality of the soul may be considered as a wager, a choice each human being makes on the ground of a complex set of considerations, experiences and feelings wherefrom he or she draws his or her conclusions. And yet among the various rational proofs of the existence of the immortal soul, one is particularly interesting. It will be expounded through the words of a letter written by 'Abdu'l-Bahá to Forel:

> The consummation of this limitless universe with all its grandeur and glory hath been man himself, who in this world of being toileth and suffereth for a time, with diverse ills and pains, and ultimately disintegrates, leaving no trace and no fruit after him. Were it so, there is no doubt that this infinite universe with all its perfections has ended in sham

and delusion with no result, no fruit, no permanence and no effect. It would be utterly without meaning... this Great Workshop with all its power, its bewildering magnificence and endless perfections, cannot eventually come to naught. That still another life should exist is thus certain, and, just as the vegetable kingdom is unaware of the world of man, so we, too, know not of the Great Life hereafter that followeth the life of man here below.[8]

The best result in the life of all those who have made a wager on the existence of the immortal soul is a faith in the fact that human beings always have in front of themselves a better future, guaranteed by a progressive development of the infinite spiritual capacities whereby their immortal souls are intrinsically endowed, a development that is possible only on condition that they be willing to struggle for its realization. Whereas those who have made a wager that the soul does not exist, or that it is mortal, usually come to the opposite conclusions. Since they do not have confidence in the development of the power of love whereby the human soul is potentially endowed, they uphold that 'human beings are incorrigibly selfish and aggressive' and war is one of their inevitable expressions. This 'falsehood' has created a lamentable 'paralysis of will'[9] regarding peace among the peoples.

According to the spiritual conception of the nature of reality, the spiritual nature of human beings is their essence, so that, in Khavari's words, 'we are spiritual beings, presently in a physical form,' or 'spiritual beings who are presently passing through a physical existence as part of their eternal spiritual journey.'[10]

Contradictions of human life

Human beings are therefore bound to feel a strong tension within themselves between their material or animal and spiritual nature. On the one hand, they are in thrall of physical reality, which conveys to them any individual diminution in the form of very unpleasant feelings, and which demands to be satisfied, very often with awkward urgency and, if unchecked, at any cost. This is their material or animal nature, that is, 'the insistent self, the evil promptings of the human heart,'[11] with all its emotions, abstract when compared to the body, but certainly dependent on and conditioned by the body, because its foundations are undoubtedly to be found in the brain. On the other hand, they also feel something within themselves which urges them to make efforts aimed at bending their body and insistent self towards diverse directions of love, peace and selflessness. This is their spiritual nature. Therefore, there exist in them both a strong disposition to subordinate the entire universe to their insistent self and an opposite need to love their neighbor, a tension between the urgency of taking and the need of giving, between self-protection and self-sacrifice, between the attraction towards sensible reality and towards spiritual reality, between love and hate, war and peace. 'Not in any other of the species in the world of existence is there such a difference, contrast, contradiction and opposition as in the species of man.'[12]

The rational faculty is the instrument capable of acting as an intermediary between these two poles. Whenever human beings avail themselves of it to only comply with the needs of their body and its emotions, their lives are ruled by the 'the evil ego,' the metaphorical 'Satan'[13] of Judaic, Christian and Muslim Scriptures. They remain captives of the world of nature to which they are bound because of their body. And they are like animals, because their natural emotions prevail in their lives and they therefore manifest mainly their material or animal qualities. The Scriptures say that such human beings are dead. They are alive in the physical level, but in the spiritual plane their life has really had no beginning, because they have not yet begun to express the potential spiritual virtues infused in their soul.

On the contrary, whenever, through their rational faculty enlightened by the divine teachings of the Scriptures, they take hold of their body and its natural emotions, with the intention of using them so that the virtues of their spiritual nature may emerge, they begin to live in the spiritual plane; that is, they acquire a new personal dimension, which is divine, because it belongs to a world which transcends and enlightens physical reality. This is the beginning of a real transformation, to which the Gospels and the Koran refer as 'second birth,'[14] mystical religions as second birth (*dvija*), enlightenment (*bodhi*), liberation (*moksa*) and *nirvana*, and the Bahá'í Scriptures as 'spiritual progress.'[15] The first time a human being is born into the world of nature when he or she has been conceived; the second time, he or she is born into the worlds of the spirit, as he or she becomes conscious of the qualities of the spiritual worlds and manifests them in his or her life in the form of virtues.

These concepts clarify the difference between animals and human beings. They are different from one another because human beings are endowed with the rational faculty that assists them in the following functions:

1. 'to discern the truth in all things,' arriving at 'valid conclusions' and 'the verities of existence';[16]

2. 'to discover the secrets of creation,' to 'safeguard and protect himself… provide and surround himself with all that scientific skill can produce';[17]

3. to discover 'that which is right,' and to arrive at 'the choice of good or evil';[18]

4. 'to know and recognize the one true God,' and to apprehend 'the divine teachings';[19]

5. to get rid of 'all the fetters of self' and 'to ascend to the pure heaven of sanctity';[20]

6. 'to render effective the will of God and give it material station';[21]

7. to acquire and manifest 'the bounties of God, that he may establish the kingdom of God among men and to attain happiness in both worlds, the visible and invisible.'[22]

Therefore, whereas for the animals the highest possible perfection is the happiness and the well-being achieved through their sensorial perception of the material world, for human beings the greatest perfection is a joy achieved in their perception of spiritual reality in the world and within themselves through the acquisition of virtues.

The Nature and the Role of Religions

Human greatness and limitations

The prevailing opinion today is that the rational faculty is a sufficient guarantee and instrument for human life, and that human beings do not need anything else for their progress. Khavari writes:

> The grand delusion of the mind is the faith it has in itself, as the unerring litmus test for everything. The rational faculty is the engine of this grand delusion. A vast universe of phenomena that mystify the logical mind is simply tagged as chaos. Hiding behind the walls of logic and objectivity, the mind illogically assumes that its capability is infinite and its pronouncements are infallible.[1]

This idea is quite common even among people who are not 'narrow-minded materialists,'[2] and who prefer to generically call themselves secularists or humanists. Among them the Italian journalist Arrigo Levi describes his faith in humanity as a

> faith in the creative power of the human spirit, which does not need any Supreme Guarantor, any outer justification, beside its own existence and survival, so that it may overcome the innumerable defeats it had to meet throughout the centuries.[3]

However, the limitations of the rational faculty are quite evident. The narrowness of the rational faculty is manifest even in its most distinguished fruit, the natural sciences. This faculty leads human beings to a quite accurate knowledge of material reality. Nevertheless, whenever the meaning and the value of certain truths are to be understood, and more comprehensive perspectives are to be achieved, or unifying theories formulated, the rational faculty very often misses the mark, as is obvious when the history of science is studied. Many theories were first considered indisputable, and then, after further and deeper studies, proved to be false, and were discarded.

The limitations of the rational faculty become even more evident when the applications and uses of science are considered. It appears inadequate because science requires, in its applications and uses, standards of value, or criteria establishing what is good and what is bad. The rational faculty cannot formulate a standard of universal values to be followed for the good of individuals and society, nor wholly explain the meaning of that standard, or the reasons why it should be observed. The Italian Islamist and Iranist Alessandro Bausani (1921-1988) writes: 'humankind by itself—as it is demonstrated by the same history after the so called liberation of man from eteronomous moral—cannot discover a valuable law (the number of people who were killed by human beings who chose an "autonomous moral" is far greater than the number of all the possible victims of all possible inquisitions and Holy Offices all together…).'[4] If this were not the case, we would not stand today, after a century, which undoubtedly relied on the guidance of rational faculty, on the verge of an ecological catastrophe.

Guided and restricted in their understanding by their own sensory perception, human beings are handicapped in grasping the spiritual realities of the transcendent world. It is almost impossible for them to achieve a comprehensive understanding of the nature of spirit as well as of their own soul, their position in the great creative plan of God, the purpose of, and the laws governing their existence, the direction of their development, and the process of their growth. Through their rational faculty, human beings progress at most on a merely intellectual and material plane. This is the case with the contemporary Western world, where the rational faculty, released from the fetters of past superstitions and at long last used in freedom, has made so many useful discoveries. A material civilization was born, which, on the one hand, is conducive to material well-being, but, on the other, is laden with dangers for all humankind, inasmuch as it is blind to the spiritual truths and deaf to the values with foundation in those truths.

Last but not least, human beings are able to recognize through their rational faculty the dark aspects as well as the luminous qualities of their nature, but they do not possess the forces required so that the former may be mastered and the latter manifested.

An awareness of these limitations is beginning to loom in the Western world. Giddens wonders: 'How shall we justify a commitment to reason in the name of reason?' And he adds:

> Modernity turns out to be enigmatic at its core and there seems no way in which this enigma can be 'overcome.' We are left with questions where once there appeared to be answers... A general awareness of the phenomenon filters into anxieties which press in on everyone.[5]

And Minois ascribes the responsibility of the recent efflorescence of a new 'religiosity bereft of a precise content, of an act of faith,' which he considers 'a defeat for the rational spirit,' to the fact that 'rationalism, be it of believers or of non-believers, failed to give a valid explanation of the world and specially to assure stable and acceptable cultural values.'[6]

Thus it seems evident that human beings are in need of an external and superior guidance, which may assist them in advancing comprehensive views of reality, in elaborating standards of values, in discovering and understanding spiritual reality and motivations for their struggle against the dark side of their nature—a guidance which may bestow upon them the required forces, so that they may conquer in themselves the binding power of nature and manifest the spiritual nature which is potentially hidden within them, in other words, so that they may achieve that 'spiritual progress' which 'Abdu'l-Bahá describes as 'the awakening of the conscious soul of man to perceive the reality of Divinity.'[7] All religions say that this external and superior guidance comes from a divine Master, who bestows teachings fulfilling these goals. They are the founders of the universal religions that the Bahá'í Scriptures call Mani-festations of God.

The founders of universal religions or Manifestations of God

The Manifestations of God recorded in history are Abraham, Moses, Krishna, Zoroaster, the Buddha, Jesus, Muhammad and, recently, the Báb and Bahá'u'lláh.

We may understand these mysterious personages better if we examine the common aspects of their human experiences. They came from different social backgrounds, none of them attended any school, none of them availed himself of worldly power. They always appeared in times of moral decline and announced to their people a message in the name of a Creator God Whose mouthpiece they proclaimed themselves to be.[8] Their messages have always urged human beings to transcend the limitations of their earthly life and to pursue a spiritual goal, for whose attainment the Manifestations have recommended them to follow the universal law of love, despite any sacrifice this attitude could imply, warning them that spiritual growth or decline would be the result of either obeying or disobeying that law.

In the beginning, a mere handful of disciples follows this new Master, giving rise to a scandal among the 'right-thinkers,' observant of the traditional rules. This scandal raises storms of persecution against the Manifestation and His followers. However, despite their often violent deaths and the murder of many of their early followers, their ideas, which are at first strongly opposed, eventually, show their power of renewal, transform society and usher in a new civilization.

Their teachings therefore, unlike the teachings of philosophers, conquer humankind through their intrinsic power and, when they are put into practice, prove themselves fruitful and give birth to flourishing civilizations. However, in the course of time these teachings lose their effectiveness and, according to the universal law of evolution, having yielded their fruit, they decline. This decline is caused by the corrupting influence of our material or animal nature, which, as Khavari points out, 'extends far beyond the immediate life of the person and into the very fabric of human endeavours.'[9] A number of religious leaders subdued by their material or animal nature impose wrong interpretations of Scriptures and day after day transform a dynamic spiritual teaching into a collection of dogmas, harmful to the development of humankind. It is then that a new Manifestation appears announcing a new message and new teachings so that humankind may achieve a new spiritual life. The cycle of the ages proceeds in its endless motion even in the case of historical religions which, like any other phenomenal reality, are born, grow, yield their fruit and decline.

The Manifestations of God are characterized by two distinctive features. On the one hand, we have their teachings. Initially set forth by words and then codified in the form of one or more Scriptures, they are offered as the essence of the spiritual laws that are fit for humankind in its specific stage of growth, with the promise that, if humankind complies with them, it will obtain good fruits. On the other, we have their spiritual power, which they promise to bestow upon all those who of their own free will consciously follow their teachings, so that they may be gradually transformed into creatures endowed with many spiritual virtues and capable of great attainments in the world.

The threefold reality of the Manifestations of God

According to the Bahá'í Scriptures the Manifestations of God have a threefold reality: material, human and spiritual.

Their material reality is their body, which like the body of any human being, is born, grows and dies.

Their human reality is their soul, the seat of their individuality as well as rational faculty. In this respect the Manifestations of God are, on the one hand, similar to human beings, and on the other, wholly different from them. They are similar to human beings because, since they are endowed with a soul, they have a special individuality as any human being. Thus although they are all conjoined in their manifesting a single universal divine

Reality, yet they differ from one another in their individual characteristics. They are wholly different from human beings, in that the rational faculty enables human beings to know the qualities of things, and not their essence. Moreover human knowledge is always acquired through experience or learning. On the contrary, the rational faculty of the Manifestations of God enables them to know the essence of things and not only their qualities. It is not 'a power of investigation and research,' like that of any ordinary person, but a 'knowledge of the being,' a kind of 'innate conscious power.' Therefore the Manifestations of God do not come to know reality through a learning process, they have an intrinsic consciousness of the essence of things, which is very similar to 'the cognizance and consciousness that man has of himself.' In other words, the Manifestations are conscious of the essence of things, in the same way as human beings are conscious of all their sensations and physical faculties, sentiments and spiritual conditions. Last but not least, in the Manifestations of God the expression of the rational faculty of the soul through the instrumentality of the brain does not produce, like in human beings, a limited mind, wherefrom the self in its worse and limiting aspects is generated, but engenders a 'universal divine mind.' Therefore the Manifestations of God are free from the limitations of the dark impulses of the material or animal nature of man.[10]

Their divine reality is a relationship to the divine realm that is qualitatively and fundamentally different from that possessed by human beings. They are like perfect mirrors which reflect the attributes and perfections of God, with a constancy and power that is apparent to pure-hearted people and that gives them the spiritual power required to change things as they will. Prophetic religions[11] like Christianity, Islam and the Bahá'í Faith call this divine reality the Word of God, the Logos. It is divine and eternal, and yet it is inferior to God in His Essence, because it is created by God, whereas God is uncreated.

Since the Manifestations of God have a perfect conscious knowledge of the material and spiritual worlds, they can reveal to humankind as much of spiritual reality and divine will as human beings can understand and use in that moment. These are their teachings that 'Abdu'l-Bahá, in this regard, defines as 'the science of reality.'[12]

As to their spiritual power, it is an emanation of God Whose manifestation they are. Bahá'u'lláh writes that they are 'the Vehicle for the transmission of the grace of the Divinity Itself'[13] and 'Abdu'l-Bahá explains:

> The greatest power of the Holy Spirit exists in the Divine Manifestations of the Truth. Through the power of the Spirit the Heavenly Teaching has been brought into the World of Humanity... everlasting life has come to the children of men... the Divine Glory has shone from East to West and... will the divine virtues of humanity become manifest.[14]

The relations among the Manifestations of God

In their mutual relations the Manifestations of God can be viewed in two different perspectives: the stations of unity and distinction. In the perspective of their general function, they are all the same, each of them is the mouthpiece of God and as such he is the depository of the 'Most Great Infallibility' and 'unto no one is given the right to question His authority.'[15] Whosoever does so seriously jeopardizes his or her possibility of spiritual growth, like a tree shut out from the sun. In the perspective of their specific function, 'each and everyone of them hath been the Bearer of a specific Message... and entrusted with a divinely revealed Book.'[16] Each of them reveals different qualities. In this stage they are different from one another. In fact divine revelation through the Manifestations of God is an eternal phenomenon. Revelations come one after the other as succeeding stages of a progressive phenomenon. And the law of evolution operates also in the succession of the Manifestations of God on earth. In the divine revelation, there are evolutionary cycles whereby a fruit appears, through successive stages, from a seed. Each of the Manifestations of God is a stage in this process and the teachings they bring are progressive. This progressiveness may be likened to the different brightness of sunlight in the different hours of a day, or to human spirit appearing with different powers in the embryo, the newborn baby, and so on through the various stages of human life, or to the spirit of growth which is present in the seed but manifests itself in different ways in leaves, flowers and fruits.

The Manifestations come into the world one after the other, even as springtimes follow one another, year after year. After springtime summertime comes, when the civilization ushered in by the Manifestation of God attains its greatest flourishing. Then autumn comes, when its fruits are gathered, but at the same time its decline begins, because 'taken captive by "the insistent self,"' religions themselves can change 'into man-made dogma, ritual, clerical privilege and sectarian quarrels.'[17] Finally winter comes, when only 'the dogmas and blind imitations' remain. These winters are the phases of religious decline, of the triumph of fanaticism which in its turn is the direct cause of the victory of materialistic forces, which find their origin and the confirmation of their theories in the mistakes perpetrated by the followers of religions. At that time 'again the cycle begins and a new springtime appears.'[18]

The purposes of the Manifestations of God

The Manifestations of God have a twofold purpose: to promote the spiritual growth of individuals and to further the progress of society.

The Manifestations of God come to the world to bestow spiritual education upon human beings. They help them to understand the spiritual worlds, to conceive a yearning to acquire the spiritual qualities of those worlds, and at the same time they teach them how they can achieve that goal and become emancipated from the fetters of the instincts and passions of their material or animal nature. Bahá'u'lláh writes concisely that the purpose of the Manifestations of God is 'to endue all men with righteousness and understanding, so that peace and tranquillity may be firmly established amongst them.' He compares their teachings to the mythical 'Elixir':[19] the latter transforms copper into gold, the former transforms the material or animal nature of human beings into their spiritual nature. And 'Abdu'l-Bahá explains that they intend to establish among human beings 'the bond of a love which is indissoluble,'[20] and defines their teachings as 'the science of the love of God.'[21]

The first purpose fulfils also the second: furthering the progress of society, that is, 'to carry forward an ever-advancing civilization,'[22] 'unifying humanity and establishing universal peace,' founding 'divine civilization.'[23]

As they have a twofold purpose, two aspects can be identified in their religion. The first aspect concerns the spiritual progress of the individual and of society, through ordinances that, since they concern spiritual reality, are changeless and eternal, and may be summarized as the law of love. The second function deals with the material development of society through teachings that, since they concern material conditions, subject to supersedure and transformation, change in accordance with the time, place and condition.

Proof of the Manifestations of God

Since the issue of the infallibility of the Manifestations of God is the kernel of religion, prophetic religions list a series of 'proof' on whose ground one may establish whether a self-styled prophet is a true Messenger of God. Three kinds of such proof are described: the fulfillment of former prophecies, the deeds of the Manifestations of God and the influence of their teachings.

Prophecies, worded in an obscure, often ambiguous, language, whose interpretation is quite difficult, do not seem so important, so much so from the standpoint of a rational approach to this issue.

Deeds are certainly more important, not so much their so-called miracles, convincing only to incidental eye-witnesses, as their behavior. The Manifestations of God lead a life of utter consistency with what they teach. In particular they show great strength and endurance under tests and trials.

Their teachings, known through their Scriptures, are a very important proof. They are one of their fruits and since they are in complete accord with the human needs of the age, they are a vital demonstration of the soundness of the claims of the Manifestations of God as Divine Teachers of humankind. In Jesus' words:

> Beware of false prophets, which come to you in sheep's clothes, but inwardly they are ravening wolves.
> Ye shall know them by their fruits. Do men gather grapes of thorns, or figs of thistles?
> Even so every good tree bringeth forth good fruit; but a corrupt tree bringeth forth evil fruit.[24]

The influence of the teachings of the Manifestations of God seems to be their soundest proof. Men and women, who had been weak and helpless, grow into heroes and heroines; the ignorant become learned; enemies change into friends; evil-doers turn into holy persons. The history of all religions is rich in such examples. But in the course of time the influence of the teachings of the Manifestation becomes manifest in other ways as well. The inspiration of their faith generates artists, scientists, and statesmen. A new vital and luminous civilization flourishes. Previous limitations are overcome and new goals achieved in every field.

Denial of the Manifestations of God

The Manifestations of God are seemingly frail creatures, as any human being, and yet they are the bearers of teachings which are iconoclastic in their disruptive influence on time-honored traditions, traditions which in the long run have become obsolete. No wonder, then, that they have always been rejected and persecuted by their contemporaries, or that at the beginning it is so difficult for most people to accept their teachings and recognize their station. That is part of the rules of the game of human spiritual growth. This growth is a process that rests upon a free and conscious choice between a concrete and alluring, sensible reality, and a spiritual reality which is not easily perceived and appreciated. In fact how could such a choice be free, and such a process achieve its educational purpose, if the signs of the Manifestations of God and of the spiritual worlds were evident and attractive to human eyes, that is, to that same material or animal nature that must be conquered and overcome? Or if those signs were easily grasped by human rational faculties, which are requested to independently put themselves at the service of the Manifestation? It is the human soul's attraction towards the worlds of the spirit that must be the guide of human beings, so that they may recognize the reality of the Manifestation of God, despite any obstacle raised by their material or animal nature with its dark passions and by their rational faculty with the prejudices it may easily fall prey to.

The role of religions

In conclusion, one of the fundamental assumptions of the materialistic conception of the nature of reality is that human civilization has grown through the unaided efforts of human beings, without any direct intervention of God, and that religions, dogmatic and superstitious as they are, are a by-product of human minds, and were not very important in the development of this civilization. On the contrary materialists generally see religion as having been an obstacle to civilization. According to the spiritual conception of the nature of reality, the Manifestations of God are divine teachers who offered a unique contribution to the growth of civilization, through their revelations. The power of the Manifestations of God

> has been the primary influence driving the advancement of civilization, generating legal codes, social and political institutions, artistic works, technological achievements without end, moral breakthroughs, material prosperity, and long periods of public peace whose afterglow lived in the memories of subsequent generations as imagined 'golden ages.'[25]

Without them humankind would have remained immersed in its primitive uncouthness.

Two Different Conceptions of History

Modern conceptions of history

The two materialistic and spiritual conceptions of the nature of reality imply two diametrically opposed readings of history. In the nineteenth century a number of materialistic thinkers adopted the criterion of reading history from the point of view of social evolutionism, that is, 'in terms of a "story line" which imposes an orderly picture upon the jumble of human happenings.'[1] But the forecasts they drew from their readings of history have proved to be mostly wrong. Comte announced that an ever wider and dominating industrial spirit is the most effective guarantee against any return of the military or feudal spirit.[2] Karl Marx (1818-1883) foresaw that class struggle would have unhinged capitalism and that the new socialist society would have been produced by this struggle with the same fatality which governs natural phenomena.[3] The French sociologist Emile Durkheim (1859-1917) stated that 'the further expansion of industrialism would establish a harmonious and fulfilling social life, integrated through a combination of the division of labour and moral individualism.'[4] The German economist and sociologist Max Weber (1846-1920) thought that 'material progress was obtained only at the cost of an expansion of bureaucracy that crushed individual creativity and autonomy.'[5] But none of them, says Giddens, fully anticipated 'how extensive the darker side of modernity would turn out to be.' And this dark side appeared in the establishment of totalitarian regimes, which were much more dreadful than in the past, because they connected 'political, military, and ideological power in more concentrated form than was ever possible before the emergence of modern nation-states,' in the proliferation of weapons and in the '"industrialisation of war"' with all the bloody armed conflicts that broke out in the course of the twentieth century and in the ecological disasters threatening the incipient century.[6] The successors of those thinkers did not even think to examine more deeply their materialistic premises, in order to see whether those premises could be among the reasons of their wrong forecasts. Such was their faith in those premises, that they radicalized them. And thus they came to lose any 'belief in "progress"' and to conclude that 'history "goes nowhere."' This radicalization of the assumptions of materialism, considered as one of the salient features of the end of the twentieth century, is evident, according to Giddens, in four fundamental points: evolutionistic theories and the notion that history has a comprehensible direction have been abandoned, any acquired datum can and must be constantly re-examined in the light of reason, and the world hegemony of the West is declining.[7]

A spiritual conception of history

In the spiritual perspective, history is not a casual sequence of wars, or of political or cultural events, devoid of any overall meaning and direction, but the realization of a divine plan, which is the same as God's plan for the whole creation. This plan provides for the attributes of the spiritual worlds to appear in the material world. In the specific case of human history, this plan is that humankind may arise from a pseudo-human condition, based upon the laws of the world of nature (competition and the struggle for existence with the survival of the fittest) and therefore oriented towards a quest for power, towards a more authentically human society, founded upon co-operation, universality, the consciousness of the oneness of humankind and therefore oriented towards a quest for spiritual growth through the spiritual reality of love.

The divine plan for humankind may be seen as the prosecution of the creative plan of God, which made the attributes of the spiritual worlds manifest in the material world to the point when humankind was produced. God creates the material world which produces human beings, as polished mirrors where He manifests

His qualities in the form of virtues. Each human being was born as an embryo, that is very similar to an animal, but later acquires the capacity to manifest certain divine qualities which are absent in the material world. This transformation is realized because human beings improve their ability in using their four capacities, knowledge, love, will and consciousness, whereby their souls have been endowed. This improvement is the result, on the one hand, of an intrinsic necessity and, on the other, of the help of God. God knows their inner need of perfection and responds to this need through His progressive Revelation, but at the same time leaves human beings free to respond to that Revelation at their will. History is the result of the interaction of all these factors. It is the sequence of the events produced by human beings, while they freely manifest their capacities of knowing, loving, willing and being conscious in the material world. Human beings know themselves in their material, human and spiritual natures. During this process, they leave traces of their growing consciousness. They modify the material world and create an ideal heritage which is handed down from one generation to another. Their rational faculty guides them as a light. Their love of reality moves them as an unfurled sail. Their will enables them to actualize what they have consciously known, loved and desired. In the meantime, God assists them. On the one hand, He leaves them free, so that they may learn through their mistakes. On the other, He stimulates them through His Manifestations, that explain to them which direction they should better follow in their progress, let them know a worthy object of love, and bestow upon them the required forces so that they may arise towards higher and higher levels of existence. 'Abdu'l-Bahá explains:

> Perchance, God willing, this terrestrial world may become as a celestial mirror upon which we may behold the imprint of the traces of Divinity, and the fundamental qualities of a new creation may be reflected from the reality of love shining in human hearts. From the light and semblance of God in us

may it be, indeed, proved and witnessed that God has created man after His own image and likeness.[8]

History as progress

Human history is thus a process whereby the qualities of the spiritual worlds become manifest in the world through humankind or, in another perspective, the process whereby humankind progressively fulfills the purpose of its creation: 'to radiate the Divine light and to illumine the world by his words, action and life.'[9] History is the gradual unfolding of a process of spiritualization through which humankind can freely contribute to the realization of the divine plan for creation, a process of infinite perfecting, seemingly endless before us. As Khavari writes: 'Human perfection is a process. It is a journey, not a destination.'[10]

In history progress is, on the one hand, the realization of 'a dispensation of Providence ordained by the Ordainer, the All-Wise'[11] and therefore it is necessary and inevitable. But, on the other, it also is problematic, because the course of the events is directly influenced by human actions. This implies that the course of events can develop in an infinite number of different ways whose details none of us will ever be able to forecast. It will be possible only to foresee general trends, in the awareness that perfection is an unattainable goal. In fact, as hard as human efforts may be, human beings will never perfectly manifest any quality of the divine worlds. As progressive as a civilization may be, there will always be further goals of perfection towards which humankind could advance. The concept of chiliasm, as a permanent condition of perfection, is thus obsolete.

The providential plan

There is a providential plan, the creative plan of God, which is gradual, cyclic, relative and infinite. It is a preordained plan and the Manifestations of God gradually reveal its goals to humankind. But human beings are free in their response to this plan revealed by the Manifestations of God. Having been created as free and endowed with the capacity of knowing, loving, willing and being conscious, human beings freely and consciously know, love, want and act and this is the temporal, or empirical aspect of history, which is formed by facts.

We can agree with Cardinal Carlo Maria Martini, a Bible scholar and the Archbishop of Milan, who said:

> The future lies in human freedom, as God willed it... Human freedom leads towards the oneness of all peoples, made more and more necessary because of the unbounded possibilities given to human beings to do what they want. Whether humankind will realize this oneness or not, we cannot say, but all the prerequisites are met in view of this realization... This is the strong law of history. We could stop it, but this law is stronger.[12]

According to the Bahá'í teachings, this 'brotherhood' among all the peoples of the world is 'potential... natal... intended in humanity because all are waves of one sea, leaves and fruit of one tree.'[13] Although every religion of the past was fit to become universal, human brotherhood was not realized because of human incapacity. But today brotherhood is necessary, because it is inherent in the creative Plan of God and in the capacity which has been conferred to humankind, on the one hand, by divine grace and will and, on the other, because of the consummation of a process.

Human freedom

In this process human freedom is progressive. The more human beings grow as individuals and as a society, the greater is the range of their freedom.

However, the leitmotiv of history seems to be not at the pleasure of human beings, but at God's. God has destined that humankind will mirror His image in growing perfection in the mirror of creation. This destiny cannot be avoided. As humankind is the necessary fruit of the world of creation, likewise a society founded upon the oneness of humankind is among the necessary goals of history. In the framework of this great plan, individual human freedom is preserved. If a given individual will not respond to the divine call and realize His Will as revealed by His Manifestation, other individuals will do it in his or her place. But they will do it in a different way. The overall divine purpose will be achieved, personal human goals may not be. If the peoples of the world will not make an effort to achieve the goal of the oneness of humankind, the divine plan will be delayed and humankind will go through greater trials. But finally in time the goal will be achieved.

God's freedom

Facts in time and space depend on human freedom. But the results of human deeds are not always according to the intentions of those who perform them. God realizes His great plan and mysteriously uses human beings as pawns for the realization of His purposes. All believers in God know that they cannot understand the ways through which His providential plan is realized. The divine plan remains inscrutable in its details.

The chosen people

In the old ideologies the concept of a plan of Providence was connected with the idea of a chosen people, the people of the day, the dominator, that has realized the highest idea of spirit.[14] This concept, typical of Nazi-fascism, does not belong to this spiritual conception of history. Those who consciously promote the providential plan of God are not a chosen race or group at the expense or to the detriment of others. All can cooperate for the realization of the providential plan, if they wish to. 'Abdu'l-Bahá says: 'Certain spiritual attraction is requisite in order that hearts may willingly take the step forward in the divine Cause. We must become attracted to God.'[15] All can hearken to this divine attraction which is enshrined in all hearts. 'Abdu'l-Bahá mentions a 'spiritual instinct, surely never given in vain,'[16] the 'love of exaltation,'[17] as well as the 'love of reality' which 'God has created or deposited'[18] in each human being. He says:

> In the past ages the human world has been represented as divided into two parts: one known as the people of the Book of God, or the pure tree, and the other the people of infidelity and error, or the evil tree. The former were considered as belonging to the faithful, and the others to the hosts of the irreligious and infidel—one part of humanity the recipients of divine mercy, and the other the object of the wrath of their Creator.[19]

On the contrary, all human beings are the members of the same family. All of them are 'recipients of the bounty and bestowals of God.'[20] In other words there is not one specific people that has realized the highest idea of spirit,[21] that is the most perfect and has attained salvation. There are great numbers of people who have more or less deeply understood the 'concept of spirit' and bend their efforts so that what they have understood of that concept may be realized in their lives. Today it seems that 'the highest concept of spirit' is the realization of the oneness of humankind in the world through a process of mutual education and a universal effort of cooperation. The requirements in view of this task cannot be other than kindness, wisdom, tolerance, respect, moderation, mercy, compassion, etc. All these qualities imply an absolute physical, psychological and moral non-violence, an absolute respect of that individual freedom of choice in whose absence no learning and no progress are possible, as well as a concept of equality among human beings. It is the opposite of fundamentalism.

How to read the facts of history

While we examine a historical event, we are undoubtedly interested in its peculiarities and in its relationship with other events, but also it is vital that we try to understand its meaning in the framework of the creative plan of God. The traces of God can be discovered in history as well as throughout the universe. They become manifest in the spiritual meaning of events. History itself may become 'translucent with eternity,' as Bausani used to say in other contexts. Each important historical event has a weight and meaning in view of the progressive growth of humankind towards the true dignity of its station: to manifest the qualities of the spiritual worlds in the world of creation, so that a society worthy of human beings may be created, a society founded upon the consciousness of the oneness of humankind. Identifying this weight and this meaning in the facts of history is tantamount to finding the traces of God in history.

The lesson of history

These assumptions imply a shift not only in our overall interpretation of history, but also in the focus of our attention on its events. This shift does not regard only historians, but all of us, since it also influences our evaluations of personal and collective events of daily life and modifies our judgments on facts and people.

Spirit: the fundamental theme of history

Historians have always dealt with earthly affairs, such as material accomplishments, worldly riches and glories, mundane power etc. But since material reality is part of a greater spiritual reality and there is a reciprocal influence between the material and spiritual conditions of the world as well as between 'spiritual and practical requirements of life on earth,'[23] and since human beings are creatures born from the realm of nature, endowed with an intelligence and capable of evolving towards spiritual worlds, historians should also deal with the spiritual meanings of events. 'Abdu'l-Bahá says that 'man must endeavor in all things to investigate the fundamental reality.' Since 'the essential reality is the spirit,' and 'the life of man is due to the spirit,' 'we must strive to learn of it.'[24] Therefore the foremost task of historians is to identify events and trends of thought which have made it possible for civilization to better express the qualities of the spiritual worlds.

True glory

'Abdu'l-Bahá explains:

> Man must attach himself to an infinite reality, so that his glory, his joy, and his progress may be infinite. Only the spirit is real; everything else is a shadow. All bodies are disintegrated in the end; only reality subsists. All physical perfections come to an end; but the divine virtues are infinite. How many kings have flourished in luxury and in a brief moment all has disappeared! Their glory and their honor are forgotten. Where are all these sovereigns now? But those who have been servants of the divine beauty are never forgotten. The result of their works is everywhere visible. What king is there of two thousand years ago whose kingdom has lived in the hearts? But those disciples who were devoted to God—poor people who had neither fortune nor position—are today trees bearing fruit. Their banner is raised higher every day.[25]

He compares the glory of Nero with that of Peter, who was his victim; the glory of famous queens and empresses to the glory of Mary the Magdalene; the fame of Napoleon I and Alexander the Great and that of Anúshírván (531-578 AD), a just king of ancient Persia. It follows that the idea of power completely changes. Power is usually recognized as pertaining to those personages who hold the control levers of the material life of individuals and societies, because the results of their decisions become immediately manifest. However, if we consider the changes in the long run, it is evident that those personages do not exercise a decisive influence on the course of history. The Bahá'í International Community expounds this concept in its following comments on the present situation of the world:

> Despite widely prevalent opinion to the contrary, the human race is not a blank tablet on which privileged arbiters of human affairs can freely inscribe their own wishes. The springs of the spirit rise up where they will, as they will.

They will not indefinitely be suppressed by the detritus of contemporary society. It no longer requires prophetic insight to appreciate that the opening years of the new century will see the release of energies and aspirations infinitely more potent than the accumulated routines, falsities, and addictions that have so long blocked their expression.

However great the turmoil, the period into which humanity is moving will open to every individual, every institution, and every community on earth unprecedented opportunities to participate in the writing of the planet's future.[26]

True hierarchy

Therefore we can also accept a hierarchy of individuals similar to that which is usually accepted, that is, kings, heads of state, spiritual leaders, statesmen, scientists and scholars, leaders in various branches of human accomplishment, opinion leaders, etc. But this hierarchy is acceptable only if its members absolve their responsibilities according to the universal requirements of spirituality. Only those personages who have properly fulfilled their task of carrying 'forward an ever-advancing civilization'[27] may be considered as excellent. In particular, among statesmen excellence may be recognized in all those who did their utmost in order

> to win the confidence, respect, and genuine support of those whose actions they seek to govern; to consult openly and to the fullest extent possible with all whose interests are affected by decisions being arrived at; to assess in an objective manner both the real needs and the aspirations of the communities they serve; to benefit from scientific and moral advancement in order to make appropriate use of the community's resources, including the energies of its members.[28]

Otherwise none is entitled to the true dignity of a physically occupied but spiritually undeserved rank.

Reformations

Since history is progress, reformations are quite important in view of the development of civilization. If there were no political, social, economical and other reformations, there would be neither change nor progress. Undoubtedly the most important reformations are those in the intellectual field, in the conceptions of the nature of reality. This kind of reformations enable human beings to go beyond previous conceptions, grown obsolete, and to conceive the required practical reformations. 'Abdu'l-Bahá says:

> The important factor in human improvement is the mind. In the world of the mind there must needs be development and improvement. There must be reformation in the kingdom of the human spirit; otherwise, no result will be attained from betterment of the mere physical structure.[29]

This reformation is very similar to the 'paradigm shift'[30] described by the American historian of science Thomas S. Kuhn (1922-1996), that is, a shift in 'a social construction of reality, a belief system that prevails in a certain scientific community.'[31] In Kuhn's opinion any 'paradigm shift' implies radical changes in the way of seeing things and therefore great possibilities of progress. Likewise, the shift in the materialistic paradigm that prevails today in the West could be the source of great progress. The Bahá'í International Community writes in this regard:

> Spiritual and materialistic conceptions of the nature of reality are irreconcilable with one another and lead in opposite directions. As a new century opens, the course set by the second of these two opposing views has already carried a hapless humanity far beyond the outermost point where an illusion of rationality, let alone of human well-being, could once be sustained. With every passing day, the signs multiply that great numbers of people everywhere are awakening to this realization.[32]

The modern world has often indiscriminately accepted reformations. New is good, says a fashionable slogan. But in reality not all reformations are adequate or based upon sound assumptions or bearers of good fruits. Therefore it is quite important to establish certain general standards on whose ground we could judge whether a reformation is good or not.

'Abdu'l-Bahá mentions three fundamental standards. The first is that good ideas produce practical results. He wrote:

> Many ideas rise up in the human mind; some of them concern truth and some untruth. Among such ideas those which owe their source to the Light of Truth will be realized in the outward world; while others of a different origin vanish, come and go like waves on the sea of imagination and find no realization in the world of existence.[33]

The second is that good ideas produce universal and lasting fruits:

> In this world we judge a cause or movement by its progress and development. Some movements appear, manifest a brief period of activity, then discontinue. Others show forth a greater measure of growth and strength, but before attaining mature development, weaken, disintegrate and are lost in oblivion. Neither of these mentioned are progressive and permanent.
>
> There is still another kind of movement or cause which from a very small, inconspicuous beginning goes forward with sure and steady progress, gradually broadening and widening until it has assumed universal dimensions.[34]

The third is their timeliness. According to 'Abdu'l-Bahá:

> [i]n every century a particular and central theme is, in accordance with the requirements of that century, confirmed by God.[35] In this illumined age that which is confirmed is the oneness of the world of humanity. Every soul who serveth this oneness will undoubtedly be assisted and confirmed.[36]

Therefore

> [a]ny movement which brings about peace and agreement in human society is truly a divine movement; any reform which causes people to come together under the shelter of the same tabernacle is surely animated by heavenly motives.[37]

Historical events are therefore judged by history itself: in their fruits and permanence. Facts which produce enduring fruits of peace, harmony, justice and unity among human beings are the fundamental evidences of a good reformation.

One cannot, at this juncture, avoid mentioning one of the most urgent reformations that are being discussed in these days in view of the promotion of peace, harmony, justice and unity among human beings: the reformation of the Organization of the United Nations. It has been presented by Secretary General, Kofi Annan, at the special meeting of the General Assembly on reform, held in New York on 16 July 1997. The aim of this reform is for the UN to reflect 'changes in geopolitical realities,' become 'flexible and adaptable,' reach 'across sectoral lines and institutional boundaries' and to make 'optimum use of our resources, either human or financial,' so that it may accomplish its vital tasks, that is,

> [t]o foster, restore, and build peace in all corners of the globe... [to promote] social progress and better standards of life in larger freedom... [to promote] democracy and international law as the pillars of peaceful relations among States... to establish clear norms and practices of international cooperation... [to champion] the advancement of women, and... [bring] relief and shelter to refugees... to ensure that the needs of children—the most vulnerable of all the world's people—come first.[38]

Therefore human history may be viewed as a process of progressive spiritualization whose incoming goal is the birth of a society founded upon cooperation and characterized by 'the spiritual as well as social and political unity of mankind.'[39] This goal will be sooner or later achieved. The times and circumstances of this achievement depend on human deeds and decisions in this regard. The present is thus connected with the past, where we may find the roots of the remotest human spiritual development. At the same time, the present is projected towards a better future and therefore it is quite stimulating and galvanizing. Each human being plays an important individual role in the realization of the creative plan of God. These elements of the spiritual conception of history contribute to raising in the hearts of each human being the desire to offer his or her contribution, as small as it may be, to the establishment of a future world civilization and enable each of them to give meaning to their life.

A Spiritual Conception of Progress, Development and Modernism

Human progress

If human beings are composed of body, mind and soul, the meaning nowadays mostly ascribed to the word progress is rather incomplete, because it takes into account only the material and intellectual aspects of life, while ignoring the spiritual aspects. Whereas history unequivocally testifies to an undeniable material, intellectual as well as spiritual progress of human civilization.

Material progress

Science describes the stages through which the human body evolved before taking on its present form, a form which seems to accomplish its functions so well. These stages are analogous to those through which each individual passes in the womb of his or her mother, that is, from conception to emergence from the darkness of a narrow matrix into the light of this wide world. This concept has been summarized into a biological law, the biogenetic law set forth by the German zoologist Ernst Heinrich Haeckel (1834-1919): '*ontogeny* or the development of the individual is a short and fast repetition (recapitulation) of *phylogeny* or evolution of the species to which that individual belongs.'[1]

The study of the material progress of the human body, that is, of its evolution, has caused inflamed disputes within the Christian world between evolutionists and creationists. The former upheld the primacy of science and said that science has proved that human beings descended from animals and that they are animals endowed with high intelligence. The latter upheld the primacy of religion and said that human beings have been created by God and there is no close relationship between them and the animals.

The upholders of the spiritual conception of the nature of reality may tackle this discussion in a different perspective. On the one hand, they should not forget that science has proved that the human body has gone through several transformations in the course of the ages. On the other, they should also remember that the main features of a human being are not only the form of his or her body, but also the rational power of his or her human soul that makes him or her different from any other living species. On the ground of these two assumptions, a conciliation between the recent scientific discoveries and the statements of the Scriptures may be achieved. The transformations of the form of human body through the ages, which Scriptures do not seem to deny,[2] have enabled human beings to improve their capacity to manifest the qualities of their soul, until a more perfect conformation of the brain enabled them to manifest their rational faculty.[3] At the beginning, the form of the human body was quite different than at present. It was a phase of incubation similar to that through which each human being passes while developing in the womb of his or her mother. This phase came to an end as soon as a more perfect conformation of the brain enabled the human body to manifest the rational faculty. That was the beginning of human intellectual and spiritual evolution. However, in the course of this lengthy evolution, the spiritual reality of human beings, that is, their soul, has always been a human soul.

Materialists deny the existence of the soul. Therefore they say that as long as the body has not acquired a specific form, we cannot speak of 'human beings.' For this reason they uphold the moral legitimacy of abortion. The upholders of the spiritual conception of the nature of reality defend the existence of the soul and therefore they think that a human being is always a human being, independently of the stage of development, that is, the shape, of his or her body. Therefore any ancestral protozoon was a human being, although its form was quite different from the form of a modern human being, as any human zygote is a human being, although its form is quite different from the form of the future baby. But none can deny, whatever his or her conception of the nature of reality may be, that a human zygote is *only and totally* human from the instant of its conception. In fact, if a human zygote will be left alive, it will develop into a human being, and nothing else. Likewise, on the ground of the biogenetic law formulated by Haeckel, all the direct material descendants of any primal human protozoon are not animals, but human beings. Therefore all those ancient protozoa, the direct ancestors of human beings, were human beings and therefore they were different from other protozoa, direct ancestors of animals, which may have been very similar to them in their form. And what was that difference? Human protozoa were animated by a human soul, although they were not capable of manifesting all the qualities of their soul. Animal protozoa were not animated by a human soul. This concept cannot be either proved or refuted through the methods used by natural scientists. But our rational faculty can understand it. It will either refute or accept it depending on the materialistic or spiritual assumptions which it has chosen to adopt.

The locution 'human material progress' should be used only to refer to this stage of human collective and individual development. Usually, however, it is used to denote the development of the material aspects of a civilization, that is, sciences, technology, trades, wealth, the arts, a progress which, in this context, could be better termed as intellectual progress.

Intellectual progress

Neither the materialists nor the upholders of the spiritual conception deny that humankind has made intellectual progress in the course of history. This fact is proved by the various civilizations which appeared one after the other, and whose remnants are precious documents of this extraordinary evolution that led humankind to the 'modern civilization' with its unprecedented scientific and technological development. But the materialists and the upholders of the spiritual conception differ from one another in their ideas on the causes and factors of this evolution. According to the materialists, this evolution is due to a gradual and constant improvement in the use of the rational faculty. According to the upholders of the spiritual conception it is due to a twofold set of events. On the one hand, the passing of time has implied a collective growth of humankind, which may be compared to the growth of any individual human being, and this growth has become manifest as a constant improvement in the use of all human intrinsic capacities, including the rational faculty. On the other, a recurrent intervention of God in the affairs of the world through His Manifestations has guided, inspired and strengthened humankind to use their improving physical and rational faculties. The Manifestations of God have taught and inspired, on the one hand, moral principles or values, and on the other, virtues representing indispensable factors of intellectual progress. They also have bestowed upon human beings the required spiritual powers so that they may rise towards higher standards of life than in the past.

The materialists say that these moral principles and virtues are the product of the rational faculty, independent of any religious influence. Anderson writes that '[m]orals are not being handed down from the mountaintop on graven tablets; they are being created by people out of the challenge of times' and reminds us that the Swiss psychologist and pedagogist Jean Piaget (1896-1980) and the American psychologist Lawrence Kohlberg, which he considers the two 'main [psychological] sources of contemporary work on moral development,' have described 'human beings as social animals who develop systems of morality as naturally as they eat and breath.'[4] Others, like Arrigo Levi, enthusiastically describe a secularist, or humanistic, or philosophical faith, that is, an unfailing faith in man, in his 'instinct of love,' which they consider as 'the projection of an instinct of solidarity deeply rooted in human nature and primal instincts,' whose traces may be identified 'in the maternal instinct... the clan instinct,' and finally in 'love of one's neighbor... inherited from the most remote past.' 'Intelligence, the primary feature of human beings,' he says, 'gives universal and philosophical dimensions [to this instinct of love] and makes it the one and fundamental answer to the issue of the survival of the species.'

Levi considers his own faith as 'a daughter neither of God nor of reason, which cannot justify it,' but 'as a mysterious, uncaused search after a meaning of things, after a purpose of events which we, as individuals and as a kind, live and produce, which we want to govern and by which we do not want to be governed.'[5] It is a sign of faith in human conscience and in an assumed inborn human capacity to distinguish between good and evil and to chose good more often than evil. This capacity has supposedly assisted human beings in their formulations of moral standards, which are thus the results of their reflection, rather than of a divine revelation, as all religions say.

The upholders of the spiritual conception of the nature of reality maintain, on the contrary, that without the assistance and the inspiration of the teachings of, as well as the spiritual powers bestowed by, the Manifestations of God those principles and virtues would have remained hidden and unattained for the human race. According to them, the three Zoroastrian commandments—good thoughts, good words and good deeds—the solemn 'ten words' of Moses, the inspiring words of Jesus' Sermon on the mountain, and the moral teachings of all religions cannot be the fruit of human conscience. On the contrary, human conscience is the fruit of the divine knowledge taught by the Manifestations of God, absorbed by human beings and deposited in such deep strata of their memory that it almost seems an inborn asset.[6]

We can certainly have faith in each human being today, in his or her 'instinct of love,' only because this instinct has been trained by the Manifestations of God in the course of the millennia, and this trained instinct has so deeply pervaded our culture that receiving an atheistic education is not enough to get rid of it. In reality, the failure of the attempts to uproot the religions, methodically made by atheistic governments for long decades in this century, have proved that not even a number of generations of atheistic education are enough to eliminate this deep religious stratum from our conscience. The moral and spiritual teachings of the Manifestations of God are engraved in the hearts of any human being grown up within the context of civilizations influenced by a revealed religion. But what would happen to a child grown up among animals, and thus deprived of any contact with those civilizations? Experience seems to answer that they would grow according to an imprinting received from the animals which trained them, and would be forever deprived of any possibility of apprehending human languages, perhaps not even the erect posture. According to the upholders of the spiritual conception of the nature of reality, all of us would have remained in the same level, if we would have been deprived of any relation with the spiritual worlds through the Manifestations of God. Moreover, if our civilization would have grown through the unaided efforts of our rational faculty, its development should have been more or less steady in the course of the ages. On the contrary, 'the mode of change appears saltatory and intermittent,'[7] an alternation of relatively long periods of stagnation and ages of rapid revolutionary changes. These sudden accelerations in the development of civilizations usually occur immediately after the appearance of one of those spiritual Masters.

Spiritual progress

The progressive acquisition of spiritual virtues and the adoption of nobler moral standards, which indicate spiritual progress, are a rather controversial aspect of human progress. Most materialists paradoxically uphold that in this regard human progress has been irrelevant and that human beings have fundamentally remained the same in their worst aspects. This is how they explain the persistence of conflicts and wars which characterized human history till the present day and which, in their opinion, will always characterize it. In the issue of human spiritual progress two aspects should be distinguished. The first aspect concerns the insurmountable limitations of human nature. Human beings are imperfect and their imperfection is an intrinsic part of their nature. They will never attain perfection in any of their potential virtues. The second aspect concerns their perfectibility. As to this aspect, the attitudes of the materialists and of the upholders of the spiritual conception of the nature of reality inevitably differ. The former think that human beings belong to an animal species and therefore they will always remain under the sway of their instincts and thus of selfishness and aggressiveness. The latter think that human beings are quite different from animals, because their distinctive feature is their soul, the development of whose endowments is the whole purpose of human life. This is the foundation of their trust in human perfectibility. In their opinion, the evolution of the human species and the history of human civilization demonstrate the progressive unfoldment of the capacities of the soul, as a growing human capacity of manifesting the qualities of the soul in the form of knowledge, actions, feelings and words. The Manifestations of God that came one after another in the course of history have guided humankind towards a deeper understanding of spiritual reality and an increasingly perfect moral capacity. From the concept of the existence of God and the awareness of good and evil taught by Adam, to the concept of the unity of God taught by Abraham, from the concept of the due observance of the 'law of God' which Moses 'founded' to 'the attainment of supreme human virtues through love'[8] suggested by Christ, to the union of a people and the founding of a nation upon the divine law taught by Muhammad, humankind, guided by these 'agents of one civilizing process'[9] has passed through various phases in its knowledge of spiritual reality and in its manifesting it through its actions and undertakings. We are just now emerging from a vision of spiritual reality which could be termed as mythological and entering into an era when, having attained our physical maturity and learnt how to avail ourselves of our mind, we can face the issue of spirituality in a totally new way when compared to the past. Human mind has been prepared and trained throughout the ages; today at last it is ready to attain a deeper knowledge of the mysteries of transcendency and the spiritual laws of the universe. Therefore, humankind is at long last ready to take the reins of its own spiritual development. 'It is like the birth from the animal kingdom into the kingdom of man,'[10] says 'Abdu'l-Bahá. These words remind us of the stupendous revolutions through which human beings gradually emerged from an animal way of living, and became the creatures they are today: upright position, speech, the discovery of fire, the production of the earliest tools, agriculture, the earliest societies, etc. No wonder that the upholders of the spiritual conception of the nature of reality foresee, beyond the immediate dark horizons, a luminous future for mankind on the earth. 'This time of the world', says 'Abdu'l-Bahá, 'may be likened to the equinoctial in the annual cycle... this is the spring season of God.'[11] Therefore, the incoming age will be such as humankind 'will realize an immeasurable progress upward', and 'spiritual effulgences will overcome the physical, so that divine susceptibilities will overpower material intelligence.'[12]

A new concept of development

The concept of development takes on a different meaning in the light of the spiritual conception of the nature of reality. Development is not the transformation of a culture in view of bringing it into line with other cultural standards viewed as superior because they have implied a remarkable material progress among those people who adopted them. Development is rather the systematic diffusion of spiritual principles, sometimes called human values, in the attempt to improve the quality of human life. And improving the quality of human life does not mean improving only its material aspects. It rather means preserving the human dignity of people and helping each individual to release the potentialities inherent in the station of man. This development will enable all individuals together to create a peaceful, just and dynamic society. And since it is by now evident that all the peoples of the world are interdependent, 'the real purpose of development' is 'laying foundations for a new social order that can cultivate the limitless potentialities latent in human consciousness.'[13]

Spiritual principles, and certainly not material means alone, are the most effective instruments to promote development. Their implementation arouses in each human being their inborn yearning for spiritual and material improvement, a yearning that has been suffocated and changed into 'a passivity learned through generations of exposure to outside influences which, no matter how great their material advantages, have pursued agendas that were often related only tangentially—if at all—to the realities of the needs and daily lives of indigenous peoples.'[14] And this yearning produces a commitment which, assisted by material means, does all the rest. It bears the fruit of success, prosperity and happiness for all those who undertake it, within the practical limitations of each individual, as well as for the society to which they belong. This kind of development is certainly 'sustainable,' since its motivations are in its subjects and not in external individuals. It also is 'practicable,' since it does not aim at the immediate attainment of improbable goals of perfection, but finds contentment and joy in small practical everyday results and draws an incentive for a greater commitment from all failures.

Therefore, if development is what Esteva writes, 'a process through which the potentialities of an object or organism are released, until it reaches its natural, complete, full-fledged form,'[15] if a people or a group of people are to develop, there are three prerequisites: they should want to grow, they should formulate a practical and acceptable idea of their growth, and finally they should also obtain the required means to realize it. The spiritual conception of the nature of reality offers a valid motivation for growth, suggests a direction of growth, which will be later autonomously and efficiently specified by each group. If this conception is shared by other more advanced groups, cooperation is promoted and thus, on the whole, larger amounts of resources become available. In conclusion, this kind of vision is likely to obtain that 'involvement of the entire body of humankind in the work of its own spiritual, social and intellectual development' which is required for the overall progress of human civilization.[16]

The concept of modernism

According to the upholders of the spiritual conception of the nature of reality, the concept of modernism is related on the one hand to ideas of renewal, reformation, change, overcoming ancient dogmas, and on the other to renewal, and not abandonment of fundamental virtues and moral principles. If renewal must be constructive, we must identify the spirit of the age and introduce the necessary reformations so that its implications may be realized. The 'oneness of the world of humanity' is the 'central theme' of our age,[17] but the religions of the world, which are the most powerful instrument in view of 'unifying humanity and establishing universal peace' and founding 'divine civilization,'[18] seem incapable of promoting this unification in our days. Therefore we may easily understand the words uttered by 'Abdu'l-Bahá said is 1912: the 'reformation and renewal of the fundamental reality of religion constitute the true and outworking spirit of modernism.'[19]

The last hundred years were characterized by a substantial change in the religious scenario of the world. In the nineteenth century religious traditions seemed well established all over the world. The political, national, and international changes after World War I, together with the success of materialism, has dramatically changed this situation. On the one hand, religious hierarchies have progressively lost their temporal power, on the other, religions have been progressively substituted in the hearts of people by other forms of irreligious faith. The unfortunate results of impiety and secularism have recently convinced a great numbers of people that humanity should go back to a sincere faith in God. Religious hierarchies, that were once so self-assured that they did not even consider the possibility of re-examining their past, have been convinced by their various defeats to reflect on their past actions. This has inevitably caused some of them to consider the idea of renewal and reformation, which has brought them closer to the true spirit of modernism requiring the 'reformation and renewal of the fundamental reality of religion.'[20]

The times have ended when the dogmatic verities taught by ancient religious leaders, in conflict with scientific discoveries, satisfied people's need for truth. That today some religious leaders are willing to revise, in the light of scientific discoveries, ancient dogmatic attitudes resulting from interpretations of the Scriptures formulated in pre-scientific ages, is a significant feature of the modern age.

The times have ended when the ancient absolutistic and exclusivistic positions upheld by various religious hierarchies, perhaps justified by difficult communication and transport that kept people away from one another, could be accepted by peoples who were not mutually familiar and thus could demonize 'the others' and exclude them from the circle of their affections. The gradual change from exclusivism to inclusivistic and then pluralistic visions reveals an increasing need for spiritual unity among the peoples. And the various kinds of fundamentalism that arose since the 1970s are mostly considered 'a dying convulsion,'[21] 'desperate rear-guard actions against an inevitable dissolution of sectarian control,'[22] 'a fiercely reductive faith… a retreat from God… [an attitude] denying a crucial monotheistic theme… the ideal of compassion.'[23]

The times have ended when the personal dimension of spirituality seemed to be sufficient. The present conditions of the world suggest that today the collective dimension comes first. Although the purpose of the life of each human being is to gain self-knowledge through the acquisition of divine virtues, this acquisition is not an end in itself. Today the acquisition of divine virtues seems meaningful only in view of the personal contribution each human being can and must offer to the continuous advancement of human civilization and in particular to the realization of the oneness of humankind. For the goal of the oneness of humankind to be achieved, it is not sufficient that the individual human beings strive to follow the doctrines of personal salvation taught by some of the ancient religions. These efforts may be compared to the learning of the rudiments of language, indispensable to express one's thoughts. Today, the qualities acquired through those efforts should be used in the wider framework of the ideal of the oneness of humankind. The isolated efforts of individuals are certainly useful and commendable, as examples and incentive. However, they do not substantially modify the *status quo*, they do not go beyond the personal sphere, they do not involve the peoples and their governments in a common project in view of reorganizing the human affairs on earth in the light of the principle of the oneness of humankind. Therefore, many hope and wish today that 'the goal of religious practice' may be 'shifted from individual salvation to the collective progress of the entire human race,' with a consequent 'change of emphasis on the qualities to be acquired by each believer.' In this framework 'moral behavior... [should be] analyzed from the point of view of the achievement of human potential, individually and collectively, thus liberating the believer from the feelings of guilt so common in many religions.'[24]

Farzam Arbab, a distinguished Bahá'í personage, explains that this modern conception of religion and spirituality implies an important shift in the priorities of virtues. For example, from the point of view of the collective, justice is more important than charity and the attitudes which promote unity and solidarity are preferable to tolerance, as meritorious as the latter may be. It enlarges moreover the meaning of a number of virtues. For example:

> Love includes the abolition of social prejudices and the realization of the beauty of diversity in the human race. Detachment from the world is not taught in a way that leads to idleness and to the acceptance of oppression; it is acquired to free us from our own material interests in order to dedicate ourselves to the well-being of others.[25]

This conception numbers among virtues capacities which contribute to a smoother interpersonal interaction in community life, as, for example, the capacity 'to participate in meetings of consultation, to work in groups, to express opinions with fairness and clarity, to understand the points of view of others, to reach and carry out collective decisions.' Therefore in the modern world the qualification of 'spiritual' should be ascribed not so much to 'a human being whose greatest virtue is not to harm anyone,' but to 'social activists and agents of change.'[26] These are the best among post-modern human beings: those who make a greater contribution to the material, intellectual and spiritual progress of all humankind. Among them may certainly be numbered all those who, galvanized by the simple idea of a possible new world order, made an active contribution to the recent 'sudden efflorescence of countless movements and organizations of social change at local, regional, and international levels.'[27] In the light of this new collective dimension of spirituality, the mandate entrusted by the peoples of the world to their governments should be changed to: let all nations be united in promoting the best interests of humankind.

It seems that the salient feature of this age, which has been sometimes called 'postmodern,' may be a much desired and desirable spiritual renewal. Rediscovering the essence of all universal religious messages, above and beyond any particular teaching that could be conditioned on specific historical and social circumstances, is part of the 'postmodern' spirit, with its need to formulate a global ethic which may help the peoples of the world to inhabit in peace and harmony the space vessel Gaea. Armstrong writes: 'Human beings cannot endure emptiness and desolation… The idols of fundamentalism are not good substitutes for God; if we are to create a vibrant new faith for the twenty-first century, we should, perhaps, ponder the history of God for some lessons and warnings.'[28] It seems that many people are ready to reflect upon the statement that 'the peoples of the world, of whatever race or religion, derive their inspiration from one heavenly Source, and are the subjects of one God' and that '[t]he difference between the ordinances under which they abide should be attributed to the varying requirements and exigencies of the age in which they were revealed,'[29] because all religions of the world aim at creating love, oneness and brotherhood among human beings.

A Spiritual Concept of Success

In the reductive vision of religion which prevailed in the West in the nineteenth and in most part of the twentieth century, whereby Jesus was considered 'a cult leader,' and the Buddha and Muhammad were defined as 'wandering gurus in their times,'[1] religions supposedly preach success, prosperity and happiness of the body as contrasting with, if not to the detriment of those of the spirit. After a more careful examination, it becomes evident that this contradiction does not arise from Scriptures, but only from later interpretations of their words.

The spiritual conception of the nature of reality suggests a broader idea of the human being in comparison to the materialistic conception. In the framework of the latter, human beings are viewed as animals endowed with intelligence and therefore only as a body and a mind. In the framework of the former, human beings are viewed as a body, a mind and a soul. This idea of a threefold nature of human beings implies a radical change in one's view of life and its priorities, and yet it does not deny the body and the mind, as well as their needs. If each human being is a body, a mind and a soul, he or she cannot disregard any of these three aspects without producing a disharmony, and thus unhappiness within himself or herself and in society. This is the case of our age, when a materialistic conception is leading individuals and collectivities to pursue material and intellectual goals, while ignoring the needs of their souls, in the illusion that happiness may be thus achieved. On the contrary, most people have realized that 'there is no one-to-one correspondence between material well-being and personal happiness.'[2]

In a spiritual perspective, a person of success is whoever has successfully accomplished, and is successfully accomplishing his or her earthly task of reflecting the divine virtues and illumining 'the world by his words, action and life' in the context where she or he happens to live. This implies for this person, on the one hand, to 'know his own self and recognize that which leadeth unto loftiness or lowliness, glory or abasement, wealth or poverty' and, on the other, to acquire wealth 'through crafts or professions.'[3] These words describe two processes that should be simultaneously promoted in our lives so that we may successfully fulfill our purpose as human beings. On the one hand, pursuing self-knowledge in the acquisition of spiritual qualities or virtues through our observance of the spiritual principles for the sake of our love of God, and on the other realizing the required conditions in view of the achievement of well-being. The two processes are not detrimental to one other, but are complementary to one another. They are two parallel educational processes that should be simultaneously pursued: the former pertains to the soul and spiritual qualities or virtues, the latter to the body and the intellect.

Acquiring spiritual qualities

We have already mentioned the threefold nature of human beings, the tension between their material or animal and spiritual natures, and the potential mediating capacity of their rational faculty, which can create and maintain a balance among those natures. The twofold educational process starts from this point: learning how to orient one's rational faculty so that it may successfully accomplish its function of making the spiritual qualities prevail upon the material or animal qualities, while carrying out the usual tasks of everyday life. It is not a matter of ignoring or repressing instincts and emotions, but of making the best use of them while observing a number of universal spiritual principles.

In the modern materialistic society this conception can come into conflict with the ideas of ethical relativism.[4] It is true that some standards of behavior change from people to people and this fact requires a pluralistic attitude. However, this is also true that all peoples share a number of fundamental principles which may be considered universal. In 1993 the Parliament of the World's Religions issued an initial document on global ethic,[5] which was signed by most of the nearly two hundred delegates of the world's religions who attended the session of the Parliament, held on the centenary of the first 'World Parliament of Religions' in Chicago in 1893. The document was the result of a two-year consultation among more than two hundred scholars and theologians representing the world's communities of faith. In this document four universal principles are identified as the foundation of a global ethic. They are: do not kill, do not steal, do not lie and do not commit sexual immorality. These four principles are further specified as four irrevocable directives: have respect for all life, deal honestly and fairly, think, speak and act in truthfulness, respect and love one another. From these directives four vital commitments are deduced: toward a culture of non-violence and respect for life, toward a culture of solidarity and a just economic order,[6] towards a culture of tolerance and a life in truthfulness, towards a culture of equal rights and partnership between men and women. These four commitments imply a willingness to subordinate the free expression of one's instincts and the satisfaction of one's desires to the more important exigencies of the above mentioned four spiritual principles. The consequence of this attitude is the acquisition of virtues, that is, spiritualization.

In the modern materialistic society, a number of people believe that this goal may be attained in the name of a 'faith in the creative power of human spirit.'[7] In a spiritual perspective, love of God represents the most effective motivation for striving to live a life in accordance with the above mentioned criteria. Love of God, as any feeling, is not easy to describe, also because it manifests itself in different forms in different human beings. The Scriptures of all religions are deeply pervaded by this feeling and their perusal is certainly very useful for all those who want to better apprehend its meaning.

One of the forms of love of God inspired by religions is love of Scriptures. The Vedas, the Bible, the Gospels, the Koran, the Bahá'í, Zoroastrian and Buddhist Scriptures comprise precious teachings for the edification of humankind, an incomparable guidance about how to live in peace with ourselves, with our fellow-beings and with the world. Most of them who are familiar with Scriptures conceive a reverent love for them and consider them as a unique source of inspiration and knowledge, a precious spiritual heritage for all humankind.

Another form of love of God inspired by religions is love of the Manifestations of God. This is not love for the human reality of those personages, but for their divine qualities and teachings. In the Gospel, for example, Jesus is described as 'the Son of the living God,'[8] come to the world to be 'the way, the truth, and the life,'[9] a dispenser of love to all those who met him, willing to sacrifice himself on the cross so that he might be faithful to his redemptive mission. The Buddha's biographies depict the Enlightened One as a man inspired by a deep compassion towards all creatures and thus capable of arousing love in those who met him, a love which prompted those lovers to follow the path of salvation that the Buddha was teaching. The teachings of all religions inspire respect and love towards the one who formulated them.

Loving the Scriptures, or the Manifestations of God, is the same as loving the divine reality which they reveal and therefore the same as loving the perfections of God. This love is meaningless when it is not manifested in behaviors that are in harmony with the contents of their teachings. The Bhagavadgita says:

> He who (behaves) alike to foe and friend, also to good and evil repute and who is alike in cold and heat, pleasure and pain and who is free from all attachment.
>
> He who holds equal blame and praise, who is silent (restrained in speech), content with anything (that comes), who has no fixed abode and is firm in mind, that man who is devoted is dear to Me.
>
> But those who with faith, holding Me as their supreme

aim, follow this immortal wisdom, those devotees are exceedingly dear to Me.[10]

Deuteronomy prescribes: 'And thou shalt love the Lord thy God with all thine heart, and with all thy soul, and with all thy might.' But it also teaches that this love corresponds to the love of God for His people and to the duty of observing His precepts: 'And these words, which I commanded thee this day, shall be in thine heart.'[11] Jesus says: 'If ye love me, keep my commandments.'[12] And Bahá'u'lláh writes: 'The essence of love is for man to turn his heart to the Beloved One, and sever himself from all else but Him, and desire naught save that which is the desire of his Lord.'[13] And he advises: '"Observe My commandments, for the love of My beauty."'[14] Therefore love of God is a feeling of the heart, which can be transformed into action. In this regard it may be defined as 'a need to act according to the law of love.'

Where does this need to act according to the law of love arise in human hearts if it is not inborn? There is in human beings an inborn need to defend their own lives, or at most the lives of their offspring, but certainly not that of sacrificing a part of what they may have, out of love for their neighbor. Religions are the instruments whereby God has gradually changed and is changing this primal human instinct of love of life into love of His Word, His Manifestations, Himself and thus into the need to act in harmony with His law, that is in its essence the law of love.

In a spiritual perspective, we will more effectively obtain the love of God and our spiritual transformation, if we make our choices and bend our efforts according to the teachings of the Manifestations of God, expounded in the Scriptures, and if we do that out of pure love. We will thus obtain the spiritual qualities or virtues which are both instruments and fruits of spiritual progress. Scriptures teach that human life is like a school. The teacher is the Manifestation of God, the text is his revealed Book, the pupils are all human beings, the lessons are the events of daily life wherefrom human beings can learn how to discover in themselves the required qualities so that they may tackle the events of life in conformity to the divine laws, that is, in conformity to virtues. Pain is sometimes a feeling of inadequacy in front of an event we still do not know how to tackle and solve in conformity to divine laws and that, in this respect, can be defined as a test. Most interpersonal conflicts are a consequence of spiritual immaturity, since those who do not yet know how to sublimate their self-centeredness into self-effacement very easily come into conflict with one another.

A spiritual path

The acquisition of spirituality is a gradual process which requires constant effort. Religious literature is rich in texts describing the stages of that process, which is often described as a path. In the Christian world the spiritual path is usually divided into three stages or ways, that are the purgative, illuminative and unitive ways. Also the texts of Sufism, Islamic mysticism, usually divide this path into three stages: the path (*taríqa*), knowledge (*ma'rifa*) and truth (*haqíqa*), that more or less correspond to the three ways of Christian mysticism. The Bhagavadgita describes three different ways: 'a knowledge of Reality (*jñana*) or adoration and love (*bhakti*) of the Supreme person or... the subjection of the will to the Divine purpose (*karma*).'[15] Among the Bahá'í Scriptures, the *Seven Valleys* by Bahá'u'lláh describe seven stages, called Valleys of search, love, knowledge, unity, contentment, wonder and true poverty and absolute nothingness.

All these descriptions are important not much because they help their readers to obtain a deeper understanding of the ways of spirituality, but mainly because they encourage them to fight their inner battles to achieve the spiritual goals they have set for themselves. It does not seem that the mystical transformation which they call for should be reserved to a few individuals who may feel a spontaneous attraction towards it. It seems, on the contrary, that if we really want to accomplish successfully our earthly task of reflecting the divine virtues and illumining the world by our words, action and life where we happen to live, each of us should be willing to face this metaphorical journey.

Bahá'u'lláh's *Seven Valleys* describes the inner changes any spiritual traveler experiences, in his or her perception of reality within himself or herself and in the world, as he or she rises up from the 'plane of heedlessness,'[16] that is, spiritual slumber, towards an awakened consciousness of his or her 'true poverty,' that is, of his or her station as a servant of God. This consciousness implies the capacity of viewing oneself as a mere instrument in view of the realization of the will of God on earth: to organize the affairs of the world under the banner of the organic oneness of humankind. Each valley describes an inner attitude which is precious for whosoever wants to pursue the spiritual path. The 'intense ardor' of the Valley of search is a providential attitude for all those who want to lay or reinforce the foundations of their spiritual transformation. The fearless devotion of the Valley of love is suited to all those who wish to strictly adhere to the ideal they have embraced. The luminous certitude of the Valley of knowledge is of great assistance for all those who have to overcome the tests of life while pursuing the spiritual goals they have set for themselves. The peaceful vision of the life of the Valley of unity is indispensable to all those who need a clear vision to direct their efforts towards their specific goals of inner perfection and unity with their fellow-beings. The bliss and joy of the Valley of contentment, the innocent amazement and perfect wisdoms of the Valley of wonderment, the utter humbleness of the Valley of true poverty and absolute nothingness are both prizes and instruments for all those who are determined to bear witness in their deeds to their love of God, so that they may radiate it towards other hearts. And these are certainly not all the meanings of this masterpiece of mystical literature of all times.

Spiritual qualities[17]

Spiritual qualities or virtues are described in great details in all Scriptures. Bhagavadgita 12:13-20, passages in the *Majjihima nikaya* or other Buddhist Scriptures describing the *Astangika-marga* (eight-fold path), the 'Beatitudes' of the Gospels,[18] Koran

2:177 and other passages of this Book or the *Hidden Words* by Bahá'u'lláh are but a few examples of these descriptions. The *Hidden Words*, a work of 'unsurpassed preeminence among the... ethical writings'[19] of Bahá'u'lláh, have been described as 'a love-song' having as 'its background the romance of all the ages—the Love of... the Creator and His creature.'[20] It is the story of an individual who from the plane of a 'mortal' and 'fleeting world,' the 'prison' of 'self,' struggle towards a condition of 'peace,' 'rest,' 'light,' and 'holiness,' identified with the plane of 'everlasting' and 'eternal life.'

The individual is encouraged to forfeit the material world and love the spiritual world, to become detached from the dark sides of material or animal nature and love divine perfections. This detachment does not imply that life on earth be abhorred, but only that it be considered in its real meaning: a school wherein human beings may come to know, in the practice of daily living, the qualities of their divine nature, and thus God himself.[21] Neither the material world nor the human self in their ephemerality are worthy of being loved. God alone deserves to be loved and this love for Him is an indispensable prerequisite for the bestowal of divine bounties, which are required for spiritual progress.

Love of God is essentially the love for His Manifestation on earth. This love is not just a feeling, or a thought. It is a continuous quest for the nearness to God and for God's 'pleasure,' pursued through the observance of His 'statutes' for His love's sake.[22] The nature of these 'statutes' is such that evidently the path towards nearness to God and His pleasure passes through the world and among human creatures. The *Hidden Words* convey a clear admonishment: 'Walk ye in the ways of the good pleasure of the Friend, and know that His pleasure is in the pleasure of His creatures.' And moreover: 'The basest of men are they that yield no fruit on earth.' This admonishment is further specified: 'The best of men are they that earn a livelihood by their calling and spend upon themselves and upon their kindred for the love of God, the Lord of all worlds.' And moreover: 'Of all men the most negligent is he that disputeth idly and seeketh to advance himself over his brother... Let deeds, not words, be your adorning.'[23] These words leave no place for doubts: all those who love God should learn how to live a life of detachment, commitment and service, for His love's sake, because loving God means loving His creatures. Spiritual growth is thus neither a barren ascetic exercise, nor a narcissistic process of self-gratification, but a path leading, through service, to the progress of humankind.

The qualities required to achieve this goal are many. Love for the Manifestation of God is primarily love for human beings and this love becomes manifest as pure intentions, justice, sincerity, righteousness, faithfulness, humbleness, tolerance, the capacity of overlooking the flaws of one's neighbour and being forgiving, of avoiding envy and malice, of being generous and sensitive to the sufferings of others and willing to assuage them. These qualities, which may be considered as acquired only when they become manifest in 'deeds of stainless holiness,' often imply for one to renounce one's personal 'pleasure.'[24] Therefore one should be able to meet the trials with steadfastness and patience and understand their meaning: an opportunity to bear witness, mainly in front of oneself, to one's detachment from the ephemeral and one's love for the Eternal. Of great help for whoever is struggling for detachment are prayer, during which a person forgets everything else but God and communes with His Spirit, drawing from it strength and inspiration, as well as a practical daily examination of one's conscience which helps in understanding one's situation, in view of better organising oneself and going ahead.

As spiritual qualities are increasingly acquired and perfected, self and passion, fear and uncertainty become less, and peace, joy, certitude and love grow stronger. One's physical, intellectual and spiritual potentialities are actualised with growing harmony and diminishing conflicts. The heart, pure in its determination of expressing its love for God in the form of deeds, has attained not only kindliness, intended as the capacity of actively loving others and of being lovable, but also radiance which transforms it into a lamp of guidance.[25] Such a person has become one of those righteous described by Bahá'u'lláh: 'Wouldst thou seek the grace of the Holy Spirit, enter into fellowship with the righteous, for... even as the true morn [he] doth quicken and illumine the hearts of the dead.'[26]

Spiritual transformation: the challenge of the modern age

The process of spiritual transformation is undoubtedly a mystical path, but a *sui generis* mystical path, because it is deeply rooted in the actions of daily life. The travellers on this path are bound towards holiness, but a holiness of this world. The practical results of their transformation become manifest in an extremely important field, their relations with their neighbours and therefore these results reach well beyond their families and private circles. They have deep repercussions in the social and political spheres. Whoever learns how to look at the self and the world not as ends, but as means to achieve qualities which may be placed at the service of humankind and thus promote its well-being, is qualified as an excellent citizen. And a society made by such transformed citizens, willing to co-operate with others, is a society worthy of human beings, creatures made in the image of God, and suited to promote the spiritual growth of all. This transformation is the challenge of the modern age.

The culmination of spiritual evolution

'Abdu'l-Bahá said that human beings are 'intelligent beings created in the realm of evolutionary growth.'[27] This definition emphasizes two typical traits of human beings: their rational faculty and their capacity for growth. Led by their rational faculty and their 'love of reality'[28] to follow the guidance of the Manifestation of God, human beings grow not only on the material and intellectual, but also on the spiritual plane. And thus they fulfill the purpose of their creation: to carry on the evolutionary process of the material world whose universal heirs they are. The individual carries on the evolutionary process of the macrocosm both within his or her microcosm and in the macrocosm. Primal matter bears through its evolution the fruit of the human body. A soul uses that body in order to manifest, in the material world, the qualities of the spiritual worlds where she belongs. In the course of this process the soul returns unto God and thus realizes the divine plan for her microcosm. In the course of this process the soul co-operates with other souls in view of the spiritualization of society and thus she contributes to the return unto God of the macrocosm itself.

It is a vain utopia to believe what is impossible, that human beings, imperfect as they are, may achieve a perfection which belongs to their Creator alone. But 'since,' as the Constitution of the UNESCO states, 'wars begin in the minds of men, it is in the minds of men that the defence of peace must be constructed.'[29] Therefore, having faith in an infinite perfectibility of human beings because of the spiritual potentialities of their souls, their education by the Manifestation of God and their strivings towards perfection, is a very powerful mainspring which can draw humankind from perfection to perfection, to overcome boundaries growing increasingly narrow, towards wider and wider spaces of personal and collective knowledge and virtue.

The results of a wrong choice

However, if a person decides that he or she will comply with his or her attraction towards the material world, the process follows a quite different pattern. Usually this choice depends on a failure to understand the greater importance of the spiritual worlds when compared with the material one. In particular, one may have decided to accept the idea, suggested by the materialists, that 'acquisition and self-assertion' are 'the purpose of life.'[30] On the grounds of this fundamental mistake, such a person places his or her faith in an unworthy reality and ideal and his or her deeds will mirror the qualities of that same reality and ideal. Those deeds therefore will not be conducive to individual and collective harmony and peace, justice and unity, but will manifest the law of self-centredness and struggle for existence with the survival of the fittest, typical of the animal world. Thus his or her love will not be transformed into attraction towards the perfections of God, but will be an attachment to the material world. Since this individual does not love the perfections of God, he or she will not willingly accept pain and suffering while treading the spiritual path, whose meaning he or she has not understood. In this case, pain will be both retribution for wrong choice, and an encouragement to change his or her ways. Since such a person makes no sacrifice, that is, does not struggle to become detached from the self and the world, nor make any service for the well-being of his or her neighbor, none of the spiritual qualities enshrined in his or her inner reality will become manifest. For '[o]ne of the paradoxes of human life is that development of the self comes primarily through commitment to larger undertakings in which the self—even if only temporarily—is forgotten.'[31] He or she will sink deeper and deeper into the world of creation, at whose service he or she will have put his or her rational faculty, 'God's greatest gift to man.' 'Abdu'l-Bahá says that 'daily... [will] he strut abroad with the characteristic of a wild beast,' be it 'a ferocious tiger,' or 'a creeping, venomous viper,' and soon will become 'viler than the most fierce of savage creatures.'[32]

In this condition, the qualities of the material or animal nature will emerge in that person: cruelty, ruthlessness, aggression, selfishness, as well as fear, anguish, anxieties, agony, cares; and he or she will not be able to escape them. He or she will experience the hell of his or her 'insistent self,' with its 'evil promptings' and 'carnal desires.'[33] His or her spiritual progress will stop. Of such human beings Christ said: 'let the dead bury their dead,'[34] and Bahá'u'lláh wrote that they abide in 'the abode of dust' or in the 'plane of heedlessness'.[35] Until they will abandon such behavior, they will not reach the goal intended for human beings: knowing their own true being, which is divine, through the realization of divine virtues.

These concepts may be found in ancient foundational writings of Western civilization, and yet they have been forgotten. Plato

(427-327 BC) ascribes the following words to Socrates (469-399 BC) in his Alcibiades:

> acting justly and sensibly you and the state will be acting friendly to God... And... you will act looking into the divine and bright... But looking at this you will regard and know both yourselves and your own good... Then will you act correctly and well... [And] acting thus I am willing to pledge that you will be happy... But acting unjustly, looking into the godless and the dark, then it is likely you will do acts similar to these ignoring yourselves.[36]

For this reason alienation and unhappiness are rampant in the Western world, whose peoples are paradoxically wealthy and unhappy. As Khavari points out, their feeling of alienation and unhappiness is 'not caused by material progress, it is due to the drag of spiritual stagnation.'[37]

Chance, fortune or will of God?

We cannot deal with success without mentioning the imponderable factors implied in human actions. The sense of uncertainty is typical of human nature and sometimes a cause of deep anxieties. We are all aware that events independent of our will may prevent our greatest endeavors to be successful. This fact is explained in so many different ways, that it is difficult even to hint to them. Scriptures teach that nothing is fortuitous in human life. Jesus said:

> Are not two sparrows sold for a farthing? And one of them shall not fall on the ground without your Father. But the very hairs of your head are all numbered. Fear ye not therefore, ye are of more value than many sparrows.[38]

And the Koran says: 'Say: "Nothing will happen to us except what God has decreed for us: He is our Protector": and on God let the believers put their trust.'[39] Statements similar to these may be found in all Scriptures. In a spiritual perspective, chance and fortune do not exist. Everything has a meaning and a cause. Sometimes we understand them, sometimes we do not. Sometimes we can find a remedy in case of a loss, or a failure, or a defeat, sometimes we cannot. But we can always do one thing. We can avoid losing heart and change a difficulty into an opportunity, always trusting in the help of God and always ready to accept His will.

What is His will in this respect? It seems that the 'will of God,' in this respect, is whatever happened or is happening in our life independently of our choice. Therefore each of us begins his or her material, intellectual and spiritual life under the banner of the will of God. None of us has consciously and willingly chosen his or her birth place and date, the parents from whom he or she was born, or his or her early education experiences. Moreover for several years each human being is not yet in the full possession of his or her capacities of knowing and willing and therefore he or she is continuously exposed to experiences of far-reaching consequences in the face of which his or her freedom of choice is quite limited. It seems that each of us begins his or her spiritual adventure on earth endowed with a God-given, predetermined, psycho-physical asset. As such, that asset is undoubtedly the best instrument for the development of his or her spiritual nature. This attitude of trust in God and submission to His will is a powerful means of progress. It assists us to struggle so that we may transcend our limitations, which we usually experience during adolescence and sometimes consider unacceptable, wholly trustful that the required struggle to transcend them, as painful as that may be, will be very useful to our spiritual growth.

In a spiritual perspective, it is better for us, on the one hand, to accept in radiant acquiescence whatever came, comes or will come from Him and, on the other, to take wise and determined actions on whatever we can improve, within ourselves and in the world at large, in the light of His teachings. Therefore we should love action, but not its results. The Bhagavadgita teaches: 'do thy work as a sacrifice, becoming free from all attachment.'[40] This well-balanced detachment from all things gives us the required courage so that we may accept our failures and the necessary determination so that we may go on and struggle towards success.

The meaning of failure and loss, and the consequent pain and suffering, is explained in all Scriptures. 'Abdu'l-Bahá points out three fundamental meanings pertaining to this. Pain assists human beings in perfecting through the struggle they are obliged to fight to put things right. It assists human beings in gaining better self-knowledge through the expression of those spiritual qualities which are required to implement the remedy and which are part of their spiritual nature. It finally helps human beings to become detached from the material world of whose ephemerality they are an evidence.

Spirituality and poverty

The threefold, material, intellectual and spiritual commitment of human beings is strongly influenced by social conditions. Most people think that ideas of spiritual development are of little value in extremely unfavorable social conditions. According to the upholders of the materialistic conception of the nature of reality, the reconstruction of those social conditions has priority over any spiritual development in the conviction that 'the satiation of the appetites' may be conducive to 'the exhaustion of greed' and 'the moral perfection of humans.'[41] None can deny that such reconstruction is urgent. But, in view of that reconstruction, the reconstruction of the spiritual conditions is also extremely urgent. It is urgent in those parts of the world where its great wealth could be quite effectively used in the struggle against poverty, and where 'the satisfaction of the appetites' has apparently whet the appetites, selfishness and 'greed.' But it is also urgent in those areas where social conditions are unfavorable, since the development of the intellectual and spiritual qualities of their inhabitants would be very useful in the implementation of wise development projects. In fact it is evident that no development project for an area can be successful without the active participation of its inhabitants. In other words, if they do not become its responsible subjects, long-term development will not take place. Evoking this active participation is part of a process of spiritual development, which implies the acquisition of a greater self-consciousness. Therefore, since spiritual progress and development imply the acquisition of such important virtues, they are effective and urgent everywhere.

A Spiritual Concept of Prosperity

The ideas of the upholders of the materialist and the spiritual conceptions of the nature of reality are quite different also on the concept of prosperity. The former focus their attention only on its economical connotations and think that it can be realized merely through material means and social and political reformations. The latter say that prosperity comprises both economical and spiritual well-being and therefore cannot be realized if a number of spiritual or moral principles are not implemented. There is also another fundamental difference between the two groups. According to the former, economical well-being is an end in itself, according to the latter it is only an instrument for developing 'human abilities' and achieving 'human well-being in the full sense of the term,'[1] that is, material, intellectual and spiritual well-being. Consequently, the former unreservedly praise Western civilization, which is undoubtedly characterized by a remarkable material well-being, the latter wonder whether Western peoples, who 'have not advanced to the higher planes of moral civilizations,' accumulate terrible weapons and fight bloody wars, are really entitled to 'lay claim to a real and adequate civilization?'[2] As a matter of fact, at the beginning of the twenty-first century the optimistic promises of well-being of the materialists have not been fulfilled. International peace has not been established, the cultural achievements of humankind are still unavailable to great masses of humanity, and the economic gap among the peoples is growing wider and wider. Many agree with Giddens that

> it seems difficult to suppose that the disparities between rich and poor countries could be reduced through further

global industrialisation on a large scale. Not only would such a process produce a still greater deterioration in global ecology, sufficient resources simply do not exist for the world's population to adopt ways of life comparable to those of the First World societies.[3]

Facts demonstrate that pursuing material well-being while disregarding spiritual values is the cause of many ills, a possible factor of war and unhappiness.

1. It promotes the competitive struggle for existence and inhumanity towards each other.

2. It favors the most aggressive individuals and therefore it encourages that resources and power come concentrate in their hands.

3. It penalizes those who are willing to abide by spiritual principles and therefore implies that resources and power tend to be concentrated in the hands of people who act against spiritual principles.

4. Since it penalizes those who are willing to abide by spiritual principles, it encourages immorality.

5. Since it implies that resources and power tend to be concentrated in the hands of aggressive and morally unscrupulous individuals, it favors armed conflicts.

6. It favors self-centeredness and therefore it jeopardizes interpersonal relations, even those among the members of the same family, and a healthy family is very important for the growth of a society.

7. It favors permissivism and therefore it weakens the moral fiber of people, which is a vital factor for material progress itself.

8. It favors all sorts of excesses, penalizes moderation and therefore creates an imbalance in all fields of life, particularly the environment.

Therefore the common definition of prosperity as 'a state of high general economic activity marked by relatively full employment, an increasing use of resources, and a high level of investment,'[4] is incomplete, because there is no true prosperity without spiritual well-being.

In the spiritual perspective, prosperity depends on two important sets of factors: on the one hand, the adoption of sound principles, methods and forms of political life, and on the other, the implementation of a number of universal principles or values by individuals and government institutions.[5] These values were synthesized by Hossain B. Danesh, Dean of the International University of Landegg (Switzerland), as follows: 'unity in diversity, the harmony of science and religion, the equality of men and women... the eradication of prejudices of all kinds, the preservation of human rights, and the promotion of justice and freedom—in short,... the assertion of the fundamental nobility of every human being and the ultimate victory of the human spirit.'[6] These values are the most important spiritual prerequisites of prosperity.

Spiritual prerequisites of prosperity

Unity in diversity: love and the removal of competition

All Scriptures offer eschatological visions based on the triumph of good, that is, love, over evil, that is, hate. More than three thousand years ago the Zoroastrian Scriptures foresaw the final triumph of Good in a day when 'shall Evil cease to flourish, while those who have acquired good fame shall reap the promised reward.'[7] In the eighth century BC, Isaiah prophesied a time when 'they shall beat their swords into plowshares, and their spears into pruninghooks.'[8] In the seventh century AD, the Koran promises a time when 'in gardens of bliss.... no frivolity will they hear... nor any taint of ill, only the saying, '"Peace! Peace!"'[9] Bahá'í Scriptures refer nowadays to those promises in terms of fulfillment and state that that fulfillment depends on a huge collective effort aiming at creating a society inspired by the concept of the organic oneness of humankind. In this vein the Bahá'í International Community remarks:

The unifying effect of the twentieth century revolution is nowhere more readily apparent than in the implications of the changes that took place in scientific and technological life. At the most obvious level, the human race is now endowed with the means needed to realize the visionary goals summoned up by a steadily maturing consciousness.[10]

These goals, sometimes defined 'kingdom of God on earth' may be today envisaged as 'the emergence of a global civilization in which the development of the whole range of human potentialities will be the fruit of the interaction between universal spiritual values, on the one hand, and, on the other, [the great] material advances' already achieved today.[11]

Evidently, such an enterprise has been hindered by two mighty obstacles. The first obstacle is 'a deep-seated conviction of the inevitable quarrelsomeness of mankind... [which] has led to the reluctance to entertain the possibility of subordinating national self-interest to the requirements of world order, and in an unwillingness to face courageously the far-reaching implications of establishing a united world authority.' The other obstacle is 'the incapacity of largely ignorant and subjugated masses to articulate their desire for a new order in which they can live in peace, harmony and prosperity with all humanity.'[12] As to the former, a few authorities raised their voices against this lamentable mistake from the scientific world. The anthropologist and paleontologist Richard Leakey has shown the absurdity of such an idea, given the fact that 'any species which was genetically programmed for intraspecific aggression would have been eliminated by natural selection within a few generations. Indeed one can hardly imagine a more negatively selective gene than one that inclines anyone who carries it to destroy everybody else who carries it.'[13] As to the latter, the Bahá'í International Community remarks that a number of recent important developments, such as 'the accelerating extension of education to the masses,' 'the information technology explosion,' and 'a profound shift of consciousness' whereby among other things many people 'have come to know, with deep certainty, that true fulfillment is as much a matter of this world as it is of the next,'[14] have at least partially modified this condition. This change begins to transpire in the 'sudden efflorescence of countless movements and organizations of social change at local, regional, and international levels.'[15] A clear sign of this efflorescence comes from the 'Millennium Forum Declaration and Agenda for Action Strengthening the United Nations for the 21st Century,' whose opening words are:

> 1,350 representatives of over 1,000 non-governmental organizations (NGOs) and other civil society organizations from more than 100 countries, have gathered at the United Nations (UN) Headquarters in New York from 22–26 May 2000 to build upon a common vision and the work begun at civil society conferences and the UN world conferences of the 1990's, to draw the attention of governments to the urgency of implementing the commitments they have made, and to channel our collective energies by reclaiming globalization for and by the people.[16]

Most people wonder, together with the Bahá'í International Community, 'how much more suffering and ruin must be experienced by our race before we wholeheartedly accept the spiritual nature that makes us a single people, and gather the courage to plan our future in the light of what has been so painfully learned.'[17]

In a spiritual perspective, the most effective instrument in view of establishing the oneness of humankind is the development of the soul's loving capacity. This development, which is one of the foremost results of spiritual progress, implies two important consequences. On the one hand, it lessens and finally eliminates the competitive struggle, which is fundamentally a struggle for power upon the others. A remnant of the animal life in human society, the competitive struggle creates tensions and distrust and is a factor of unhappiness, since it forbids all those who practice it to achieve the noblest quality which a human being may acquire, undemanding love. The materialists maintain that this struggle is indispensable in view of material progress, and that in its absence individuals become deprived of initiative and lazy. The upholders of the spiritual conception of the nature of reality observe that 'ever since the seeking of preference and distinction came into play, the world hath been laid waste. It hath become desolate,'[18] and that 'the struggle for existence is the fountain-head of all calamities and is the supreme affliction.'[19] They remark that they who love God want to do all things in the best way, in the observance of spiritual principles, which are an efficient guarantee of morality, even of love among human beings. They maintain that the need of achieving excellence in all things is a sufficient guarantee of spiritual, intellectual and material progress, independently of the competitive struggle, which is unworthy of human beings. On the other, the development of the loving capacity implies not only the capacity of seeing each human being as a temple of God, precious in his or her unique individuality and therefore worthy of the greatest respect and support in the free expression of his or her capacities and qualities, but also the willingness 'to take up, consciously and systematically, the responsibility for the design of their future'[20] together with all other human beings.

Education and harmony between science and religion

That knowledge bestows upon the peoples of the world a greater share of control over their own destiny and new means for their collective prosperity is an idea shared by most people, and therefore it does not need any discussion.[21] Universal education is undoubtedly among the most important prerequisites of prosperity. But education should comprise both the 'two basic knowledge systems through which its [human consciousness] potentialities have progressively been expressed: science and religion.'[22] Thus a balance will be promoted between science and religion, a balance which is an important factor of prosperity, since it avoids two typical conditions of the lack of civilisation: superstition, born from religious fanaticism, and materialism, born from the prejudices into which the upholders of science may fall. The former is well known. But we find very few comments on the prejudices of those upholders of science, who 'fail to maintain a critical distance between themselves and their own beliefs.' They are the 'fanatical secularists,' expounders of dogmatic secularism, which has been described as 'religious dogmatism turned upside down... modernity without a sense of humor... a faith in human rationality not yet deflated by a healthy dose of skepticism.' The most fanatic among them, like the 'Jacobins of Revolutionary France and the Communists of the Soviet Union are ample testimony to the fact that intolerance and inflexibility are no more acceptable when they are motivated by lack of religion than when they arise from a conflict between religious beliefs.'[23] However, very often this dogmatism passes unnoticed. And, as the Bahá'í International Community observes, at the end of the twentieth century although

> for the vast majority of the world's population, the idea that human nature has a spiritual dimension—indeed that its fundamental identity is spiritual—is a truth requiring no demonstration... [however] most of the priorities—indeed most of the underlying assumptions—of the international development agenda [have] been determined so far by materialistic world views to which only small minorities of the earth's population subscribe.[24]

A shift in this attitude—that is, a greater objectivity while teaching the present fundamental ideas of the materialistic conception of the nature of reality which are presently taught as incontrovertible verities, the introduction of programs of spiritual and moral education in the schools and a greater concern for the spiritual and moral teachings of all the universal religions of the world, not only from religious people but also from intransigent as well as moderate secularists—could be of great advantage in view of the prosperity of humankind.

The equality between men and women

For long centuries and in most cultures women have always been considered inferior to men and required to abide by the will of the males. This has caused the rights of half of humankind to be curtailed and has contributed to the perpetuation of conflict among human beings. Since women occupy a vital position in society, as mothers and the first educators of their children, and since their typical qualities of greater sensitivity, tenderness, mercy, sympathy, receptivity, mental alertness, abnegation and loving capacity are extremely important for the elimination of all conflicts from, and the pacification of society, women need to be recognized everywhere as equal to men. Without this recognition society will be collectively harmed, because it will be deprived of the precious qualities of many women, which are indispensable for the establishment of a durable international peace. 'Abdu'l-Bahá said in 1912:

> The world in the past has been ruled by force, and man has dominated over woman by reason of his more forceful and aggressive qualities both of body and mind. But the balance is already shifting; force is losing its dominance, and mental alertness, intuition, and the spiritual qualities of love and service, in which woman is strong, are gaining ascendancy. Hence the new age will be an age less masculine and more permeated with the feminine ideals, or, to speak more exactly, will be an age in which the masculine and feminine elements of civilization will be more evenly balanced.[25]

The elimination of prejudices

Among the many results of education there is also the elimination of prejudices, that is, the elimination of ancient wrong beliefs, harmful to peace and cooperation among peoples. They comprise racial, national, social, religious prejudices, that is, the tendency to consider one's race, nation, social class, religion as superior to the others. These prejudices are a factor of conflicts and therefore of unhappiness. Their elimination can contribute to the reconciliation of the peoples of the world and thus to the prosperity, peace and happiness of the human world. It would take too long examining each of them, pointing out their irrationality and nefarious consequences, and suggesting ways and means to eliminate them. We will be satisfied with a hint about religious prejudice.

Religions have always played a primary role in society. Although in the course of the twentieth century they have seemingly lost part of their prestige, yet they are present in the hearts of most people. This fact on the one hand has positive effects, through all those who have understood that love and brotherhood among human beings is the most important law of each religion and therefore bear witness to this law in their behavior. But on the other it also has negative effects, through a persisting fundamentalist and fanatical attitude which, because of the conflicts it arises, 'is undermining not only the spiritual values which are conducive to the unity of mankind but also those unique moral victories won by the particular religion it purports to serve.' Therefore it is very important for religious leaders to 'submerge their theological differences in a great spirit of mutual forbearance that will enable them' to 'work together for the advancement of human understanding and peace,'[26] to co-operate among them for the establishment of those moral principles which represent the most precious heritage of their religions and to promote that free and independent search after truth which is the starting point of any true spiritual progress. Without this unity among religions, and this open-minded attitude within each religion, religious conflicts will continue and there will be no collective happiness.

Defending human rights and promoting justice and freedom

'Abdu'l-Bahá said: 'When freedom of conscience, liberty of thought and right of speech prevail—that is to say, when every man according to his own idealization may give expression to his beliefs—development and growth are inevitable.'[27] The respect of human dignity requires that each individual may express the potential qualities with which he or she has been endowed and use them for the service of society. In view of this goal to be achieved, society should take the responsibility of guaranteeing a number of fundamental rights and freedoms, such as 'universal education, freedom of movement, access to information, and the opportunity to participate in political life... freedom of thought and belief, including religious liberty, along with the right to hold opinions and express these opinions appropriately,' and especially the 'freedom to investigate the purpose of existence and to develop the endowments of human nature that make it achievable.'[28] Since 1948, when these rights were enunciated by the United Nations Organisation in its Universal Declaration of Human Rights, great progress has been accomplished. However, these indispensable freedoms are seemingly no more guaranteed by 'the ideology of partisanship that has everywhere boldly assumed democracy's name and which, despite impressive contributions to human progress in the past, today finds itself mired in the cynicism, apathy, and corruption to which it has given rise.'[29] A wise reformation of the present political order is needed so that it may become imbued with more authentically democratic and less conflictual spirit and methods.

Modern society is characterized by an unequal and iniquitous distribution of wealth and a remarkable difference in the levels of the social and economic development of its various peoples. This situation keeps a large part of the world population in a condition of subjection and obvious unhappiness. It moreover causes continuous conflicts which are an obstacle to collective happiness. It is vitally important that the peoples of the world reorganize together, in peace, all national and international, political, social and economical affairs, so that the conditions may be gradually realized whereby all humankind may achieve that 'happiness of the world of humanity, which is the ultimate aim.'[30] In the same vein the 1995 World Summit for Social Development stated in its Declaration and Plan of Action that human rights, democracy and freedom—which are essentially moral and spiritual values—are the foundation of social and economic development.

The nobility of each human being and the victory of the spirit of man

From the spiritual standpoint, a human being is noble when his or her spiritual nature dominates his or her material or animal nature. This happens when he or she complies with spiritual or moral principles. Thus his or her spirit conquers the forces of nature. Spiritual or moral principles, which are vital for individual spiritual development, are also vital for a harmonious social life. They may be compared to the rules by which the traffic becomes acceptably organized and disciplined even in the most chaotic metropolis. Traffic-lights, right-of-ways, one-way streets, the convention of keeping to the right (or left) are simple rules whose adoption has enabled increasing numbers of vehicles to more easily circulate beside one another in conditions of relative safety. The same is true in the case of spiritual or moral laws. Their observance makes interpersonal relations, which are the foundation of social life, to work more easily. Consider, for instance, the waste of energy in political or commercial relations and transactions, in view of the fact that a number of people do not comply with the spiritual or moral principles 'do not steal' and 'do not lie.' A dialogue between two people who can trust one another is undoubtedly easier and more profitable. However, a number of politicians persist in following Machiavellian methods and a number of merchants prefer to resort to craftiness and deceit rather than to honesty, with the results we all know. And those who want to find a remedy to this situation often fall into the trap of a conflict approved by the upholders of the materialistic vision of the nature of reality, and resort to '[d]ebate, propaganda, the adversarial method, the entire apparatus of partisanship that have long been such familiar features of collective action.'[31] And yet the nobility of man requires a new method for a peaceful resolution of problems, a method which may be entirely free of conflict. Among the Bahá'ís this method is known as consultation. Consultation is characterised by a number of fundamental elements: an atmosphere of candour and courtesy, the capacity of transcending one's point of view, the belief that suggested ideas belong not to any individual but to the group as a whole, the willingness to support the decisions arrived at, and to take up, discard, or revise previous decisions as seems to best serve the goal pursued.

Social conditions of prosperity

As the spiritual requirements of prosperity are being achieved, also its social conditions are realized. Those conditions are many. Only some of them will be briefly described.

A wise and just government

The concept of a wise and just government is quite broad and a detailed description of its several aspects is beyond the scope of this writing. It will suffice to say that a 'wise and just' government is a government which cares about the interests and well-being of its citizens. This is possible if those who work for the government, both politicians and administrators, are not only technically qualified in all issues pertaining to their functions, but also meet certain fundamental spiritual or moral requirements, such as trustworthiness, righteousness, honesty, temperance, self-discipline, justice, detachment, independence of spirit, sincerity, faithfulness, devotion, magnanimity, purity of intention, spirit of service, good character etc., requirements which will enable them to 'perform their duties in a spirit of true servitude and ready compliance.'[32] Politicians and administrators qualified by these attributes will certainly not avail themselves of their power for their personal advantage or as 'means to be used against others.' On the contrary they will be aware that power intended 'as advantage enjoyed by persons or groups' and as 'the ability to acquire, to surpass, to dominate, to resist, to win' is 'profoundly mistaken in theory and of no practical service to the social and economic development of the planet.' They will rather resort to the 'power of truth... [f]orce of character... the force... of unity.'[33] Obviously if these attitudes are widespread, appreciated and prized by society, it will be easier for people to vote for politicians and select administrators adorned with them. But when society ignores spiritual and moral values, and prizes the struggle for survival, this condition remains a utopia.

A just law system

'Abdu'l-Bahá writes that justice means 'to regard humanity as a single individual, and one's own self as a member of that corporeal form, and to know of a certainty that if pain or injury afflicts any member of that body, it must inevitably result in suffering for all the rest.' In the light of this definition a just system of law is 'in accord with the Divine laws which guarantee the happiness of society and protect the rights of all mankind' and insures 'the integrity of the members of society and their equality before the law.'[34] Only intellectually and spiritually progressive legislators will be able to formulate laws that meet these requirements.

A good educational system

The importance of teaching both science and religion has been already mentioned. We must now add that a good educational system will not only teach its students whatever may be profitable so that in future they may carry on a work useful for themselves and society, it will also train them to use their rational faculty freely and make good spiritual and moral choices in their daily lives.

Psychological research has proved that children learn many things through imitation. Therefore a teacher whose behavior or character are reprehensible may have a bad influence on his pupil, although he or she may teach them very useful intellectual notions. Therefore the quality of an educational system does not depend only on good legislation, but also on the quality of the teachers. They should be both intellectually and spiritually qualified people. Materialistically oriented societies, in the name of freedom, are inclined to disregard the spiritual aspects of the cultural development of their teachers. However, since the right of the children to be protected from the bad influence of reprehensible teachers is also to be taken into consideration, this issue deserves to be examined and solved.

Enlightened opinion leaders

Opinion leaders are quite important, because they represent an example, which many people will imitate, in the hope of achieving the same success as they did. Therefore, a society which prizes people who are reprehensible in their moral conduct does not promote the happiness of its members, since it encourages them to make wrong moral choices, which are an important factor of unhappiness. Therefore, among the qualities of the opinion leaders should be 'enlightenment, capacity, faith, honesty, devotion and high-mindedness,' 'diligent attention to truth and righteousness... dedication and resolve and devotion to the good pleasure of God... the desire to attract the favorable consideration of the ruler and to merit the approval of the people.'[35]

It is evident that the emergence of opinion leaders characterized by these qualities depends on many factors: good laws and a good educational system are sufficient only if education is intended as spiritual, moral, intellectual and material education. The spiritual and moral discipline required for the acquisition of the above mentioned qualities depends only on one's conscience and is more easily acquired in the green years.

An honest people

A people moved by feelings of love, friendship and unity towards all human beings and willing to cooperate with the government for the realization of its projects, moved by a spirit of religiosity, that is, of obedience to the divine law, is a vital factor of prosperity. It is evident that there is a deep interaction between individuals and society. Good individuals make a good society and vice versa, a good society makes good individuals. A struggle towards perfection is therefore indispensable both at the individual and institutional levels.

Public order

Public order, intended as a society characterized by a low level of crime and lawlessness, is a good guarantee of prosperity. It depends on many factors. The most important seems to be a widespread common and sound conception of the nature of reality, 'as it affects their relationships with one another and with the phenomenal world.'[36] In this condition interpersonal relations are easier, since even the most diverse people more easily understand one another because they understand reality in a similar way. The materialistic conception has been gradually introduced and is now generally accepted in the West. But this conception has been split up in a continuous fruitless reflection about itself, diverted from the search for truth, oriented towards the search of personal interest, and paradoxically lead into the blind-alley of a dogmatic faith in its own method which is considered infallible, and of the denial of all truth, values, and ideals. It is time for spiritual or moral values to resume their place in human hearts, so that human beings may be encouraged to follow a spiritual path which will promote their true well-being. But this will happen only if religions, which claim to be the defenders of spirituality, will comply with their own most authentic premises: respect for the freedom of the human spirit, which can manifest its God-given qualities only through an act of conscious and willing submission to the divine law of love performed out of love. This is the best guarantee of public order in a society ruled by a good government, with good laws and a good educational system.

Good international relations

In the absence of good international relations, there is always a possibility of conflict. History has demonstrated that war is ruinous. This concept became very clear during the twentieth century. This century has experienced two terrible world wars, many bloody local wars, and a prolonged condition of unstable balance between two superpowers, USA and USSR, known as the Cold War, which ended in 1987. After the end of the Cold War, peaceful resolution of conflicts has become more widespread and important than it has ever been before. Although bloody wars are still being fought, today great numbers of people are ready to work for international peace and believe it will be successfully realized.

While reorganizing all human affairs, a collective international disarmament treaty should be signed and tribunals of international arbitration invested with the authority of solving inevitable divergences which could raise armed conflicts, should be formed.

True democracy

Obviously the attainment of the prosperity of humankind requires so many changes that only a universal collective effort will be able to establish the foundations for its achievement. The Bahá'í International Community states that the protagonists of this enterpirse must be

> all of the inhabitants of the planet: the generality of humankind, members of governing institutions at all levels, persons serving in agencies of international coordination, scientists and social thinkers, all those endowed with artistic talents or with access to the media of communication, and leaders of non-governmental organizations.[37]

This universal collective participation is possible only in an atmosphere of democracy. But, as has been said, democracy cannot be identified with 'the ideology of partisanship that has everywhere boldly assumed democracy's name and which, despite impressive contributions to human progress in the past, today finds itself mired in the cynicism, apathy, and corruption to which it has given rise.'[38] And it seems that the present ideology of partisanship may make way for a more authentic democracy throughout the world only in the framework of all the above mentioned personal and collective changes.

Unity: the fundamental trait of prosperity

Globality is a very important component of prosperity. In the third millenium it is impossible to think of the prosperity of a people independently of the prosperity of others. The present conditions of the world do not allow this. The close interdependence of the peoples of the world is a recognized fact. Therefore prosperity can be conceived nowadays only in global terms. Unity is an indispensable element of any strategy for achieving prosperity. The representatives of the NGOs gathered in New York for their Millennium Forum write:

Globalization should be made to work for the benefit of everyone: eradicate poverty and hunger globally; establish peace globally; ensure the protection and promotion of human rights globally; ensure the protection of our global environment; enforce social standards in the workplace globally.... This can happen only if global corporations, international financial and trade institutions and governments are subject to effective democratic control by the people. We see a strengthened and democratized United Nations and a vibrant civil society as guarantors of this accountability. And we issue a warning: if the architects of globalization are not held to account, this will not simply be unjust; the edifice will crumble with dire consequences for everyone. In the end, the wealthy will find no refuge, as intolerance, disease, environmental devastation, war, social disintegration and political instability spread.[39]

A Spiritual Concept of Happiness

If we recognize the threefold, animal, human and spiritual nature of human beings, we also perceive their happiness has a threefold, animal, human and spiritual aspect. This is the opinion of the American psychologist Rhett Diessner, who distinguishes three levels of happiness: physical, or 'pleasure,' which 'comes from obtaining the sensory pleasures of the body'; human, or social, which 'derives from human interaction (either intrapersonal or interpersonal),' such as 'giving and receiving affection... [a] sense of belonging and acceptance from other beings... the esteem of others, and... respecting one's own skills and qualities'; and spiritual happiness or joy. We will deal with spiritual happiness only, which Diessner compares to 'the constant calmness of the deep ocean, which is unruffled by stormy waves and rain above it.'[1] Mystical literature of all times is rich in excerpts describing this spiritual condition. We will mainly refer to the Bahá'í literature.

It is permanent

This is the first feature of spiritual happiness. Since it belongs to the spiritual dimension, which is free from space-time limitations, it is permanent, whereas since physical and human happiness depend on the chances and changes of life, they are ephemeral. Spiritual happiness is described as a spiritual condition which does not depend on external conditions, but on a feeling of the heart and an attitude of the mind. 'Abdu'l-Bahá said:

> Happiness is an internal condition. When it is once established man will ascend to the supreme heights of

bliss. A truly happy man will not be subject to the shifting eventualities of time. Like unto an eternal king he will sit upon the throne of fixed realities. He will be impervious to outward, changing circumstances and through his deeds and actions he will impart happiness to others.[2]

These words do not deny that spiritual happiness is attended by the same biochemical phenomena as physical and human happiness, however they imply that it is produced by a different immediate cause. Happiness in itself, as a state of mind, is always a spiritual condition, independently of its immediate cause, because its experiencing subject is the soul, the body is only its instrument. A physical or social event is interpreted by the soul's capacity of consciousness in such a way as it produces certain biochemical phenomena in the brain which the soul perceives as 'happiness' through her mental faculties. Since the event is transient, also its accompanying biochemical phenomena and the consequent feeling of happiness are transient. As to spiritual happiness, it depends on a permanent condition of the soul which has been achieved through its spiritual transformation, which somehow can always produce and sustain in the brain the same biochemical phenomena which characterize physical and human happiness. This condition of happiness sometimes reaches a peak, that spiritual experience which most mystics have described through metaphors of human love and its climax of happiness It is the ecstatic experience.

It is a human capacity

Human happiness is also described as a potential capacity of human beings to rejoice at the gifts bestowed by the spirit. Spiritual happiness can become manifest only when it is developed. Therefore its acquisition is often gradual. 'Abdu'l-Bahá says that '[t]he star of happiness is in every heart; we must remove the clouds so that it may twinkle radiantly.'[3] These words seem to refer to the fact that spiritual happiness is achieved when 'the clouds' of the material or animal nature and its dark emotions are removed and the 'star' of the divine nature and its feelings may 'twinkle radiantly.' Khavari writes: 'Happiness and misery are emotional interpretations. We can be truly happy in the midst of terrible circumstances or be miserable in spite of having it all. The key to happiness is having a spiritual perspective on life.'[4]

The requirements of spiritual happiness

A number of requirements of spiritual happiness are described below.

Purity

'Abdu'l-Bahá says that 'God originally endowed man with an individuality which enjoyed that which was beneficial.'[5] He explains that '[t]he hearts of all children are of the utmost purity,' like 'mirrors upon which no dust has fallen' and therefore they are 'near to God.'[6] Yet, the original purity of children is because of their naive weakness. In the course of their lives, it may happen that they are enticed by their animal or material nature with its base emotions. In this case their inborn purity is lost and their souls may fall prey to 'selfish disorders, intellectual maladies, spiritual sicknesses,'[7] so that they go so far as to love harmful things and to hate beneficial things. But their development may also take quite another direction. In the course of their lives, their purity may be strengthened 'through the power of intelligence... through the great power of reason and of understanding,' so that when those children grow to manhood, they become 'pure... simple... sincere.'[8] These qualities enable them to be aware of their truest human needs, which are their spiritual needs, above their less noble, material or animal instincts. And this awareness encourages them to expose themselves to the beneficial influence of their own good deeds performed for the sake of their love of God and thus helps them to grow towards an increasing spiritual consciousness and the capacity of perceiving spiritual joy.

A Spiritual Concept of Happiness

Being open to receive the bounties of God

'Abdu'l-Bahá says that '[t]rue happiness depends on spiritual good and having the heart ever open to receive the Divine Bounty.' Then He adds: 'If the heart turns away from the blessings God offers how can it hope for happiness?'[9] This openness to receive the bounties of God becomes manifest in two main attitudes: obeying God's commandments and submitting to His will.

As has been said, a willing and conscious submission to the commandments of God out of His love implies the acquisition of spiritual or moral qualities, as for example loftiness of intentions and purposes, integrity and other virtues as well as self-respect, which *Webster* defines as 'a confidence in one's own worth as a human being and a concern to maintain it,'[10] and therefore spiritual progress, a true transformation. 'Abdu'l-Bahá says that whosoever has been spiritually changed becomes 'beloved in the sight of God, beloved in the estimation of the righteous ones and beloved and praised by the people.'[11] And then he adds:

> When he reaches this station the feast of eternal happiness is spread before him. His heart is serene and composed because he finds himself accepted at the threshold of His Highness, the One. His soul is in the utmost felicity and bliss even if he is surrounded by mountains of tests and difficulties. He will be like unto a sea on the surface of which one may see huge white waves, but in its deeps it is calm, unruffled and undisturbed.[12]

As to submission to the will of God, 'Abdu'l-Bahá says: 'Afflictions and troubles are due to the state of not being content with what God hath ordained for you. If one submits himself to God he is happy.' He relates the following anecdote:

> A man asked another: 'In what station are you?' He answered: 'In the utmost happiness.' 'Where does this happiness come from?' He answered: 'Because all the existing things move according to my wish; therefore I do

not find anything contrary to my desire; thus I have no sorrow. There is no doubt that all the beings move by the will of God, and I have given up my own will, desiring the will of God. Thus my will becomes the will of God, for there is nothing of myself. All are moving by His will, yet they are moving by my will. In this case, I am very happy.

When man surrenders himself everything will move according to his wish.[13]

Submission to the will of God and obeying His commandments imply that human beings be 'proactive,' a quality which the American writer Stephen R. Covey defines as being 'responsible for' one's life, and also as 'the ability to choose... [one's] response.' Covey writes that '[h]ighly proactive people... do not blame circumstances, conditions, or conditioning for their behavior. Their behavior is a product of their own conscious choice, based on values, rather than a product of their conditions, based on feeling.'[14] These words are undoubtedly descriptive also of all those who know that they must surrender to the will of God and at the same time never stop struggling in order to modify whatever they can modify so that the will of God, as revealed by His Manifestations, may be realized on earth.

Love of God

The most important consequence of the process of spiritualization is a growing consciousness of the love of God. 'Abdu'l-Bahá says: 'The most great, peerless gift of God to the world of humanity is happiness born of love—they are the twin sisters of the superman; one is the complement of the other.'[15]

Scriptures teach that God has created the world out of love. Bahá'u'lláh for example writes:

> Veiled in My immemorial being and in the ancient eternity of My essence, I knew My love for thee; therefore I created thee, have engraved on thee Mine image and revealed to thee My beauty.
>
> ...Wherefore, do thou love Me, that I may name thy name and fill thy soul with the spirit of life.[16]

Divine love, the cause of creation, gives life to whatever exists. 'Abdu'l-Bahá describes it as follows:

> Know thou of a certainty that Love is the secret of God's holy Dispensation, the manifestation of the All-Merciful, the fountain of spiritual outpourings. Love is heaven's kindly light, the Holy Spirit's eternal breath that vivifieth the human soul. Love is the cause of God's revelation unto man, the vital bond inherent, in accordance with the divine creation, in the realities of things. Love is the one means that ensureth true felicity both in this world and the next. Love is the light that guideth in darkness, the living link that uniteth God with man, that assureth the progress of every illumined soul. Love is the most great law that ruleth this mighty and heavenly cycle, the unique power that bindeth together the divers elements of this material world, the supreme magnetic force that directeth the movements of the spheres in the celestial realms. Love revealeth with unfailing and limitless power the mysteries latent in the universe. Love is the spirit of life unto the adorned body of mankind, the establisher of true civilization in this mortal world, and the shedder of imperishable glory upon every high-aiming race and nation.[17]

Human beings can know this love, if they become part of it in their daily lives. They can do this if they manifest this love in their thoughts, feelings, words and most of all deeds, as they strive to secure 'the peace and well-being of every individual member, high and low alike, of the human race.' Whosoever loves God makes every effort so that the light of Reality may dispel the darkness of error. This person radiates his or her love of reality as 'human perfections... qualities that are excellent and pleasing, and spiritual behavior.' And today 'Reality is the love of God. Reality is the knowledge of God. Reality is justice. Reality is the oneness or solidarity of mankind. Reality is international peace. Reality is the knowledge of verities.'[18] Therefore all those who work today with a sincere heart for the achievement of these goals promote the spirituality of the world. They directly experience and create love within themselves and all around. This divine act, which is knowledge of God as love, makes them somehow companions of their Creator and thus arouses in them a joy that is a remote reflection of the divine happiness which mystics relate to the creative act of God and which has been sometimes compared to the fresh laugh of a child. This knowledge and love of God 'is the greatest, the only real happiness, because it is Nearness to God.'[19]

Trials and pains of love

The path of spiritualization is not always easy. This is part of the educational method of the creative plan of God. For human beings to *freely* choose God as their supreme object of love and to decide to live under the consequences of this choice, they must learn how to recognize the signs of God, wherever they present themselves. In practice they must learn how to live according to His will and therefore they must learn how to follow a suitable line of conduct each time life presents them with its lessons. Therefore they must acquire first of all self-effacement, which implies the capacity of placing the altruistic demands of the divine law above one's selfish interest. Bahá'u'lláh describes this part of the process of spiritualization in the Valley of love of the *Seven Valleys*. Sufis call it the path (*taríqa*) and Christian mystics refer to it as the purgative way. In this stage spiritual seekers learn how to consider themselves as instruments at the service of the Cause of God. And what is the Cause of God? The Cause of God is the practical realization of the oneness of humankind on earth and the achievement of the happiness of all human beings. Spiritual seekers thus fulfil their purpose in the creative plan of God, because they contribute 'to render effective the will of God and give it material station.'[20] They thus become partners in the divine creative act and in His happiness. It is not difficult to understand that this process implies a struggle against one's animal or material nature and its emotions, and thus a certain amount of pain. Scriptures describe these pains as the tests of life and consider steadfastness in meeting them as a sign of true love. Bahá'u'lláh writes: 'For everything there is a sign. The sign of love is fortitude under My decree and patience under My trials.'[21]

Fear of God

As any other spiritual quality, also fear of God can assume different connotations depending on the different degrees of personal spiritual development. Is it fear of God the feeling that is experienced by primitive human beings, who have just vaguely grasped their relation with God, when confronted with the most awesome expressions of the forces of nature which they have deified? The concept of the fear of God is possibly unwelcome to modern Westerners because of these immature aspects. Armstrong writes:

> Those of us who have had a difficult time with religion in the past find it liberating to be rid of the God who terrorized our childhood. It is wonderful not to have to cower before a vengeful deity, who threatens us with eternal damnation if we do not abide by his rules. We have a new intellectual freedom and can boldly follow up our own ideas without pussyfooting around difficult articles of faith, feeling all the while a sinking loss of integrity.[22]

Certainly in the case of mature human beings, who have accomplished a certain degree of intellectual and spiritual progress, fear of God is a quite different attitude. In their case fear of God is not the cringing of a subject in front of a cruel tyrant, but the fear of a child before a parent, whose love is greater than justice. In a sense this fear of God could be compared to the awareness of the consequences of natural laws. No one would jump from the fifth floor for faster descent, well aware that the law of gravity would cause her or him to crash against the ground. And no one would certainly feel ashamed of such a fear. The same thing is true in the spiritual sphere. Breaking a divine law may not imply immediate and evident consequences, but in time it exercises devastating effects upon our souls, and thus upon our well-being. To fear God means being afraid to break His spiritual laws, for fear of consequences. This feeling is quite healthy, it is a real protection, wholly justified in a weak creature who has but a partial knowledge of reality. And in any case it is always supported by the love of

God, the experience of His attributes of love and mercy.

A good character

The word character derives from the Greek 'charakter,' which means seal and impression. In a linguistic perspective, the *Grande Dizionario* defines the Italian word *carattere*, that is, character, as 'all the psychic dispositions and natural qualities proper to an individual, which distinguish his personality from any other.'[23] The *Oxford* defines it as '[t]he sum of the moral and mental qualities which distinguish an individual or a race, viewed as a homogeneous whole; the individuality impressed by nature and habit on man or nation.'[24] And *Webster* as 'the complex of accustomed mental and moral characteristics and habitual ethical traits marking a person, group, or nation or serving to individualize it.'[25] In the psychological perspective, character is described as 'the psychic properties of a living being... the actual and specific being of a man... the indivisible (individual) peculiarity of the person..., manifest in certain specific experiences, which are organized as a whole, subject to change, while preserving their essence.'[26]

According to the Bahá'í teachings, character is the 'true criterion of humanity,' because 'the happiness and greatness, the rank and station, the pleasure and peace, of an individual' also depend on 'his excellent character.' But an excellent character is a guarantee of rank and happiness only 'on condition that its center of emanation should be reason and knowledge and its base should be true moderation.'[27] The character is excellent and acceptable in the sight of God of him who 'is adorned with the saintly attributes and character of the Concourse on High,' who conducts himself 'with trustworthiness and rectitude and... lead [a] chaste and virtuous life,' who 'close[s] his eyes to whatever he may possess, and open[s] them to the things of God... [who] cease[s] to occupy himself with that which profiteth him, and concern[s] himself with that which shall exalt the all-compelling name of the Almighty... [who] cleanse[s] his heart from all evil passions and corrupt desires.' The best instrument in view of achieving a good character is 'the fear of God... the weapon that can render him victorious, the primary instrument whereby he can achieve his purpose,'[28] victorious over his material or animal nature, of course, so that 'self-restraint' may be obtained, a virtue that Socrates himself considered as 'the very cornerstone of virtue.'[29]

It would take too long to describe all the qualities which belong to a good character. 'Abdu'l-Bahá mentions: 'justice and fair-mindedness; forbearance and compassion and generosity; consideration for others; candor, trustworthiness, and loyalty; love and loving-kindness; devotion and determination and humanity,' 'sincerity of intent,... high purpose,... purity and spotless honor,... surpassing kindness and compassion,... the keeping of... covenants... concern for the rights of others,... liberality,... justice in every aspect of life,... humanity and philanthropy,... valor and... unflagging efforts in the service of mankind,' 'to fear God, to love God by loving His servants, to exercise mildness and forbearance and calm, to be sincere, amenable, clement and compassionate; to have resolution and courage, trustworthiness and energy, to strive and struggle, to be generous, loyal, without malice, to have zeal and a sense of honor, to be high-minded and magnanimous, and to have regard for the rights of others.'[30]

A good character[31] can be taught and acquired. Training in good character means 'the rectification of qualities; arousing the desire to become accomplished and acquire perfections, and to cleave unto the religion of God and stand firm in His Laws... to be well wishers of mankind, to be kind to all.' Acquiring a good character means '[to] acquire the heavenly characteristics of the spirit, and [to] see for [oneself] beyond any doubt that there is no fiercer hell, no more fiery abyss, than to possess a character that is evil and unsound; no more darksome pit nor loathsome torment than to show forth qualities which deserve to be condemned.'[32]

Human beings of good character, with their 'qualities of extraordinary sympathy and loving-kindness,' their radiant hearts, their kind and lovable nature, are able to conquer 'the cities of men's hearts.'[33] Their relations with other people are easy and therefore they are precious in a world which is struggling towards higher levels of unity among human beings.

Spiritual happiness and wealth

It would be a mistake to think that spiritual happiness must deny wealth. When material wealth is acquired within the framework of the laws of God and when it is employed with fairness and generosity, it is a precious good. It is a source of shame and dishonor only when it is dishonestly acquired and used for selfish purposes or, God forbid, to the damage of other people. 'Abdu'l-Bahá said:

> The honor of the human kingdom is the attainment of spiritual happiness in the human world, the acquisition of the knowledge and love of God. The honor allotted to man is the acquisition of the supreme virtues of the human world. This is his real happiness and felicity. But if material happiness and spiritual felicity be conjoined, it will be 'delight upon delight,' as the Arabs say.[34]

On the contrary, since spiritual happiness implies selflessness and love of one's neighbor, a great number of spiritually happy human beings, who also are rich, creates a better society and thus a greater happiness for all. The achievement of this important goal is the reason why all Scriptures require that each human being follows the path of spiritual perfection. Khavari remarks: 'When spiritual intelligence decides the value and use of every material means, including money, we are likely to have the best of all worlds—good means to good ends, as well as personal happiness.'[35]

Spiritual happiness and society

Spiritual happiness implies that all those who have acquired it feel a deep need to share it with others and a willingness to make sacrifices in view of collective happiness. Besides, since the relationship between the individual and society is a reciprocal one, the process of personal transformation required in order for happiness to be achieved is undoubtedly favored by a happy society, that is, a society which has achieved a good standard of material and spiritual progress.

A Conclusion

Although the individual and collective conditions which have been previously described are not rampant in the world today, however the signs of the germination of the earth are even more evident at the very end of the twentieth century, when in preparation of the Millennium Summit of September 2000, the Millennium Forum Declaration has been drafted. It says:

> Our vision is of a world that is human-centered and genuinely democratic, where all human beings are full participants and determine their own destinies. In our vision we are one human family, in all our diversity, living on one common homeland and sharing a just, sustainable and peaceful world, guided by universal principles of democracy, equality, inclusion, voluntarism, non-discrimination and participation by all persons... It is a world where peace and human security, as envisioned in the principles of the United Nations Charter, replace armaments, violent conflict and wars. It is a world where everyone lives in a clean environment with a fair distribution of the earth's resources. Our vision includes a special role for the dynamism of young people and the experience of the elderly and reaffirms the universality, indivisibility and interdependence of all human rights—civil, political, economic, social and cultural.[1]

That these words have been written, that there are people who believe in their feasibility without leaping 'to the grandiose assumption that somehow we can sit down today and make tomorrow's world,'[2] and willing to struggle for their achievement, this is the most promising evidence of the germination of the planet. Only in this context can we realistically discuss human success, prosperity and happiness. Any other aspiration seems unfair. The success, prosperity and happiness of individuals are inextricably woven with one another and thus attainable only in the context of a spiritual vision of the nature of reality, conducive as it is to the drawing power of love which makes possible lofty aims.

Notes and References

Introduction

1. Guy Murchie, *The Seven Mysteries of Life*, p.563.
2. Murchie, *Seven Mysteries*, p.563.
3. *Century of Light*, p.129.
4. Cf. Kofi Annan, 'War: Foe of Development,' p.5.
5. Anthony Giddens, *The Consequences of Modernity*, p.64.
6. Walter Truett Anderson, *Reality Isn't What It Used to Be*, p.6.
7. John Huddleston, 'Another Look at Achieving Peace by the Year 2000,' *The Journal of Bahá'í Studies*, vol. 9.2 (June, 1999), p.51.
8. Anderson mentions the awareness that 'there is a human species, all of its members capable of interbreeding with all the others, but not members of different species' in his 'list of a few… ordinary ideas that most people hold' in our days (Anderson, *Reality*, p.21).
9. The Bahá'í International Community, 'The Prosperity of Humankind,' *The Bahá'í World 1994-95*, p.281.

The Materialistic Conception of the Nature of Reality

1. Anthony Giddens, *Modernity and Self-Identity*, p.155.
2. *Century of Light*, p.135.
3. Pitirim A. Sorokin, *The Crisis of Our Age*, p.71.
4. The son and appointed successor of Bahá'u'lláh (1817-1892), the Founder of the Bahá'í Faith.
5. 'Abdu'l-Bahá, *The Promulgation of Universal Peace*, p.312.
6. 'Abdu'l-Bahá, *Promulgation*, p.80.
7. Jacques Monod, *Chance and Necessity*, pp.112-3.
8. Karen Armstrong, *A History of God*, pp. 346, 378.
9. Fernando Savater, *Le domande della vita*. p.78-9. All translations from Italian are of the author.
10. Paolo Legrenzi, *La felicità*, p.14.
11. Piero Melograni, *La modernità e i suoi nemici*, p.153.
12. 'Abdu'l-Bahá, *Promulgation*, p.81.
13. 'The Bahá'í Studies Seminar on Ethics and Methodology Held in Cambridge

on 30 September and 1 October 1978. Comments by the Research Department at the World Centre,' The Universal House of Justice, *Messages from the Universal House of Justice 1963-1986. The Third Epoch of the Formative Age*, p.389.
14 On behalf of the Universal House of Justice,'Issues Related to the Study of the Bahá'í Faith,' *Bahá'í Canada*, May 1998. The Universal House of Justice is the supreme institution of the Bahá'í Faith.
15 *Century of Light*, pp.89-90.
16 Sorokin, *Crisis*, p.72.
17 Sorokin, *Crisis*, p.80.
18 Sorokin, *Crisis*, p.78.
19 'Abdu'l-Bahá, 'Tablet to Dr. August Henri Forel,' *The Bahá'í World 1968-1973*, vol. 15, p.37. 'Abdu'l-Bahá criticizes 'materialists of narrow vision that worship that which is sensed, that depend upon the five senses only, and whose criterion of knowledge is limited to that which can be perceived by the senses. All that can be sensed is to them real, whilst whatever falleth not under the power of the senses is either unreal or doubtful. The existence of the Deity they regard as wholly doubtful.' However he praises 'the materialistic, accomplished, moderate philosophers, that have been of service (to mankind).' He says that 'they are indeed worthy of esteem and of the highest praise, for they have rendered distinguished services to mankind' ('Abdu'l-Bahá, 'Tablet,' *Bahá'í World*, vol. 15, p.37).
20 'Abdu'l-Bahá, *Promulgation*, p.20.
21 Giddens, *Modernity*, p.171.
22 Roberto Giammanco, *Dialogo sulla società americana*, pp.3, 6.
23 Giammanco, *Dialogo*, pp.76, 92.
24 Giammanco, *Dialogo*, p.107.
25 Eric Hobsbawm, *Age of Extremes*, p.334.
26 Hobsbawm, *Age of Extremes*, p. 337.
27 Margaret Thatcher, quoted in Hobsbawm, *Age of Extremes*, p. 337.
28 Anderson, *Reality*, p.132.
29 The official name of the world wide Bahá'í community in its relationship with the outside world.
30 Matthew Weinberg, 'The Human Rights Discourse. A Bahá'í Perspective,' *The Bahá'í World 1996-97*, p.265.
31 Cf. William B. Provine, 'Mécanisme, dessein et éthique: la révolution darwinienne inachevée,' *De Darwin au darwinisme: science et idéologie*, p.119.
32 Anderson, *Reality*, pp.268, x, 13, 268.
33 Georges Minois, *Storia dell'ateismo*, p.560.
34 Giddens, *Consequences*, pp.46, 176.
35 It seems that few have realized that such destructive ideologies as Fascism, Nazism and Communism could, albeit temporarily, triumph in the twentieth century because of a 'willful . . . abandonment of reason on the part of a

considerable segment of the intellectual leadership of society' (*Century of Light*, p.62).

36 Anderson, *Reality*, p.187.
37 Minois, *Storia dell'ateismo*, p.535.
38 Bahá'í International Community, 'Who Is Writing the Future?,' *The Bahá'í World 1998-99*, p.266.
39 Bahá'í International Community, 'Who Is Writing the Future?,' *Bahá'í World 1998-99*, p.264.
40 Gérald Berthoud, 'Market,' *The Development Dictionary*, p.84.
41 Giammanco, *Dialogo*, p.12.
42 Sorokin, *Crisis*, p.83.
43 William James, *Pragmatism*, pp.31-2.
44 Giammanco, *Dialogo*, p.71.
45 William S. Hatcher, 'Love, Power and Justice,' *The Journal of Bahá'í Studies*, vol. 9.3 (September, 1999), p.7.
46 Sorokin, *Crisis*, p.131.
47 Bahá'í International Community, 'Prosperity,' *Bahá'í World 1994-95*, p.277.
48 Bahá'í International Community, 'Who Is Writing the Future?,' *Bahá'í World 1998-99*, p.264.
49 *Century of Light*, pp.85, 131-2, 136.
50 Anderson, *Reality*, p.269.
51 José María Sbert, 'Progress,' *Development Dictionary*, p.201.
52 Bertrand Russell, *The Scientific Outlook*, p.85.
53 Russell, *Scientific Outlook*, p.101.
54 *Century of Light*, p.89.
55 Armstrong, *History of God*, p.xix.
56 *Century of Light*, p.136.
57 Weinberg, 'Human Rights Discourse,' *Bahá'í World 1996-97*, p.272.
58 Weinberg, 'Human Rights Discourse,' *Bahá'í World 1996-97*, p.272.
59 *Century of Light*, p.59.
60 *Century of Light*, p.5.
61 *Century of Light*, p.43.
62 An example of this attitude in the Catholic Church is the Encyclical *Pascendi dominici gregis*, issued in 1907 by Pope Pius X, whom many historians consider as one of the most reactionary Popes of the modern age. This Encyclical set forth a number of ideas which appeared quite reactionary even at the times when they were expressed. As a matter of fact, it condemned Modernism, a cultural religious movement which was emerging in the Catholic world in those years in the attempt of reconciling religious faith, on the one hand, and modern philosophies as well as social and political conceptions, on the other.
63 *Century of Light*, p.63.
64 *Century of Light*, p.89.

65 *Century of Light*, p.89.
66 *Century of Light*, p.6.
67 *Century of Light*, p.90.
68 Khalil A. Khavari, *Spiritual Intelligence*, p.21.
69 Khavari, *Spiritual Intelligence*, p.38.
70 Bahá'í International Community, 'Who Is Writing the Future?,' *Bahá'í World 1998-99*, p.263.

Western Concepts of Success, Prosperity and Happiness

1 *Webster's Third New International Dictionary*, s.v. 'Success,' p.2282.
2 *Oxford English Dictionary*, s.v. 'Success,' vol. 17, pp.92-3.
3 Oliver Wendell Holmes, *Ralph Waldo Emerson*, p.260.
4 Giacomo Devoto and Gian Carlo Oli, *Dizionario della lingua italiana*, s.v. 'Successo, azioni,' p.2395.
5 *Dizionario analogico della lingua italiana*, s.v. 'Successo, azioni,' p.420.
6 James, *Pragmatism*, p.21.
7 Giddens, *Modernity*, p.211.
8 *Webster*, s.v. 'Prosperity,' p.1821.
9 *Webster*, s.v. 'Prosperous,' p.1821.
10 Salvatore Battaglia, *Grande Dizionario della Lingua Italiana*, s.v. 'Prosperità,' vol. 14, pp.705, 706.
11 *Oxford*, s.v. 'Happiness,' vol. 6, pp.1097; s.v. 'Happy,' vol. 6, p.1098.
12 Battaglia, *Grande Dizionario*, s.v. 'Felicità,' vol. 5, p.795.
13 Giammanco, *Dialogo*, p.6.
14 Legrenzi, *Felicità*, p.13.
15 Salvatore Natoli, *La felicità*, pp.250-1.
16 St. Augustine, *On the Psalms*, vol. 1, p.266.
17 *Webster*, s.v. 'Progress,' p.1813.
18 Battaglia, *Grande Dizionario*, s.v. 'Progresso,' vol. 14, pp.560-1.
19 Sbert, 'Progress,' *Development Dictionary*, p.200.
20 Sbert, 'Progress,' *Development Dictionary*, p.200.
21 Giammanco, *Dialogo*, p.93.
22 Gustavo Esteva, 'Development,' *Development Dictionary*, p.8.
23 Harry S. Truman, 'Inaugural Address, January 20, 1949,' *Documents on American Foreign Relations*, p.103.
24 Esteva, 'Development,' *Development Dictionary*, p.12.
25 *Oxford*, s.v. 'Developing,' vol. 4, p.563
26 *Webster*, s.v. 'Underdeveloped,' p.2488.
27 Piero Angela, 'Le frontiere della scienza e delle tecnologia,' *Verso il duemila*, p.144.
28 Wolfgang Sachs, 'Introduction,' *Development Dictionary*, p.4.
29 Bahá'í International Community, 'Prosperity,' *Bahá'í World 1994-95*, pp.274-5, 276.

NOTES AND REFERENCES

30 Bahá'í International Community, 'Prosperity,' *Bahá'í World 1994-95*, pp.275, 285, 275.
31 Bahá'í International Community, 'Who Is Writing the Future?,' *Bahá'í World 1998-99*, p.263.
32 Battaglia, *Grande Dizionario*, s.v. 'Modernità,' vol. 10, p.657.
33 Giddens, *Consequences*, p.36.
34 Berthoud, 'Market,' *Development Dictionary*, p.84.
35 Sbert, 'Progress,' *Development Dictionary*, p.200.
36 Sachs, 'Introduction,' *Development Dictionary*, p.1.
37 Legrenzi, *Felicità*, pp.17, 19.

A Spiritual Conception of the Nature of Reality

1 In common usage the locution 'universal religion' denotes independent religious traditions practiced throughout the world.
2 Armstrong, *History of God*, p.391.
3 On behalf of the Universal House of Justice, *Messages*, p.283.
4 Many of the ideas expounded in this and the two following chapters are expounded in greater details in Julio Savi, *The Eternal Quest for God* (Oxford: George Ronald, 1989).
5 Khavari, *Spiritual Intelligence*, p.245.
6 Theist, pantheist and deist philosophers believe in the existence of one God. Pantheist philosophers identify God with the world, whereas theist and deist philosophers believe that God transcends the world. However, according to the former God reveals Himself to humankind, according to the latter He does not.
7 Minois, *Storia dell'ateismo*, p.561.
8 'Abdu'l-Bahá, 'Tablet,' *Bahá'í World*, vol. 15, pp.40-1.
9 Murchie, *Seven Mysteries*, p.611.

Human Beings: Spiritual Creatures

1 'Abdu'l-Bahá, *Selections from the Writings*, p.256.
2 'Abdu'l-Bahá, *Paris Talks*, p.41.
3 'Abdu'l-Bahá, *Promulgation*, p.49.
4 Genesis says: 'And God said, Let us make man in our image, after our likeness' (Genesis 1:26). An Islamic tradition recites: 'He [God] created Adam in His image' (quoted in Annemarie Schimmel, *Mystical Dimensions of Islam*, p.188).
5 'Abdu'l-Bahá, *Promulgation*, p.69.
6 'Abdu'l-Bahá, *Promulgation*, pp.464-5.
7 Bahá'u'lláh, *Gleanings from the Writings*, p.260.
8 'Abdu'l-Bahá, 'Tablet,' *Bahá'í World*, vol. 15, p.40.
9 The Universal House of Justice, 'The Promise of World Peace,' *Messages*,

pp.687.
10 Khavari, *Spiritual Intelligence*, pp.27, 31.
11 'Abdu'l-Bahá, *Selections*, p.256.
12 'Abdu'l-Bahá, *Some Answered Questions*, p.236.
13 'Abdu'l-Bahá, *Promulgation*, p.287.
14 Cf. John 3:1-15; Koran 29:20.
15 'Abdu'l-Bahá, *Promulgation*, p.142. Scholars define mystical religions those religions which, like for example the religions of Hinduism, believe in an impersonal God, an Absolute to which the soul of the believer can be united, without the intervention of any mediator 'Prophet.'
16 Bahá'u'lláh, *Gleanings*, p.194, 'Abdu'l-Bahá, *Promulgation*, pp.63, 312-3, 316, 49.
17 Bahá'u'lláh, *Gleanings*, p.194, 'Abdu'l-Bahá, *Promulgation*, p.48.
18 Bahá'u'lláh, *Gleanings*, p.194, 'Abdu'l-Bahá, *Some Answered Questions*, p.250.
19 Bahá'u'lláh, *Gleanings*, p.194, 'Abdu'l-Bahá, *Promulgation*, p.61.
20 'Abdu'l-Bahá, *'Abdu'l-Bahá on Divine Philosophy*, p.117.
21 'Abdu'l-Baha, quoted in Mary M. Rabb, 'The Divine Art of Living,' *Star of the West*, vol. 7.12 (16 October 1917), p. 161.
22 'Abdu'l-Baha, quoted in Rabb, 'Divine Art,' *Star of the West*, vol. 7.12 (16 October 1917), p. 161.

The Nature and the Role of Religions

1 Khavari, *Spiritual Intelligence*, p.61.
2 'Abdu'l-Bahá, 'Tablet,' *Bahá'í World*, vol. 15, p.37.
3 Arrigo Levi, *Dialoghi sulla fede*, p.11.
4 Bausani, *Saggi sulla Fede Bahá'í*, p.204. The Holy Office is '[t]he Roman congregation established in connection with the Inquisition... in 1542 as the final court of appeal in trials of heresy... [and in] 1965 reformed... and changed ... [into] 'The Congregation for the Doctrine of the Faith' (*The Oxford Dictionary of World Religions*, p.438).
5 Giddens, *Consequences*, p.49.
6 Minois, *Storia dell'ateismo*, pp.590, 593.
7 'Abdu'l-Bahá, *Promulgation*, p.142.
8 There is an ongoing discussion on the Buddha's attitude in this regard, since most people say that he spoke in his own name and that he even denied the existence of a Creator God or of a human immortal soul.
9 Khavari, *Spiritual Intelligence*, p.45.
10 'Abdu'l-Bahá, *Some Answered Questions*, pp.218, 157, 218, 157, 218. For a more detailed explanation of these concepts cf. Savi, *Eternal Quest*, pp.87-9.
11 Religions that arise about a Prophet who reveals the divine will to which human beings should submit themselves in order to come closer to God.
12 'Abdu'l-Bahá, *Promulgation*, p.297.
13 Bahá'u'lláh, *Gleanings*, pp.67-8.

14 'Abdu'l-Bahá, *Paris Talks*, p.87.
15 Bahá'u'lláh, 'Ishráqát,' *Tablets*, p.108.
16 Bahá'u'lláh, *Gleanings*, p.74.
17 *Century of Light*, p.110.
18 'Abdu'l-Bahá, *Promulgation,* pp.363, 95.
19 Bahá'u'lláh, *Gleanings*, pp.206, 200.
20 'Abdu'l-Bahá, *Promulgation*, pp.344, 277.
21 'Abdu'l-Bahá, *Divine Philosophy*, p.171.
22 Bahá'u'lláh, *Gleanings*, p.215.
23 'Abdu'l-Bahá, *Promulgation*, pp.97, 375.
24 Matthew 7:15-7.
25 *Century of Light*, p.41.

Two Different Conceptions of History

1 Giddens, *Consequences*, p.5.
2 Cf. Auguste Comte, *The Positive Philosophy of Auguste Comte,* Lesson 46.
3 Cf. Karl Marx, *Das Kapital*, vol. 1, ch. 24, par. 7.
4 Giddens, *Consequences*, p.7.
5 Giddens, *Consequences*, p.7.
6 Giddens, *Consequences*, pp. 7, 8, 9, cf. p.8. Giddens does not mention among the features of the darker side of modernity the sad and undeniable moral decline of the West. However, among the features of post-modernity he includes 'the evaporating of the privileged position of the West' (Giddens, *Consequences*, pp.52-3).
7 Giddens, *Consequences*, p.10, cf. pp.52-3.
8 'Abdu'l-Bahá, *Promulgation*, p.235.
9 'Abdu'l-Bahá, *Paris Talks*, p.113.
10 Khavari, *Spiritual Intelligence*, p.101.
11 Bahá'u'lláh, 'Lawh-i-Hikmat,' *Tablets*, p.142.
12 Cardinal Carlo Maria Martini, quoted in Levi, *Dialoghi*, p.56.
13 'Abdu'l-Bahá, *Promulgation*, p.129.
14 Cf. Georg Wilhelm Friedrich, *Lectures on the Philosophy of History by G.W.F. Hegel*.
15 'Abdu'l-Bahá, *Promulgation*, p.250.
16 'Abdu'l-Bahá, *Paris Talks*, p.90.
17 'Abdu'l-Bahá, *Some Answered Questions*, p.188.
18 'Abdu'l-Bahá, *Promulgation*, p.49.
19 'Abdu'l-Bahá, *Promulgation*, p.454.
20 'Abdu'l-Bahá, *Promulgation*, p.454.
21 Cf. Hegel, *Lectures*.
22 Alessandro Bausani, 'Some Aspects of the Bahá'í Expressive Style,' *World Order,* vol. 13.2 (Winter 1978-79), pp.36-43.

23 The Universal House of Justice, *Messages*, p.602.
24 'Abdu'l-Bahá, *Promulgation*, pp.313, 279, 242, 243.
25 'Abdu'l-Bahá, *Divine Philosophy*, p.133.
26 Bahá'í International Community, 'Who Is Writing the Future?,' *Bahá'í World 1998-99*, pp.255, 268.
27 Bahá'u'lláh, *Gleanings*, p.215.
28 Bahá'í International Community, 'Prosperity,' *Bahá'í World 1994-95*, p.293.
29 'Abdu'l-Bahá, *Promulgation*, p.278.
30 Cf. Thomas S. Kuhn, *The Structure of Scientific Revolution*, p.111.
31 Anderson, *Reality*, p.73.
32 Bahá'í International Community, 'Who Is Writing the Future?,' *Bahá'í World 1998-99*, pp.267-8.
33 'Abdu'l-Bahá, *Tablets of 'Abdu'l-Bahá Abbas*, vol. 2, p.301.
34 'Abdu'l-Bahá, *Promulgation*, pp.43, 43-4.
35 The context suggests that the word 'century' may be understood in the sense of 'age.'
36 'Abdu'l-Bahá, *Selections*, p.114.
37 'Abdu'l-Bahá, *Promulgation*, p.97.
38 Annan, 'Secretary-General Pledges "Quiet Revolution" in United Nations, Presents Reform Proposals to General Assembly'.
39 On behalf of the Universal House of Justice, The Universal House of Justice, *Messages*, p.655.

A Spiritual Conception of Progress, Development and Modernism

1 Ernst Heinrich Haeckel, *The history of Creation of the Development of the Earth and its Inhabitants by the Action of Natural Causes*.
2 The Koran, for example, says that God created humankind 'in diverse stages' (Koran 71:14).
3 The Koran, for example, may hint to this stage as 'the best of moulds' (Koran 95:4).
4 Anderson, *Reality*, pp.259, 155.
5 Levi, *Dialoghi*, pp.28, 29, 31.
6 The *Oxford English Dictionary* defines conscience as '[t]he internal acknowledgement or recognition of the moral quality of one's motives and actions; the sense of right and wrong as regards things for which one is responsible; the faculty or principle which pronounces upon the moral quality of one's actions or motives, approving the right and condemning the wrong' (*Oxford*, s.v. 'Conscience,' vol. 1, p.754). According to the spiritual conception of the nature of reality, the sense of right and wrong, which is the foundation of our conscience, is the fruit of the process of spiritualization promoted by the teachings of the Manifestations of God.
7 Ervin Laszlo, *Evolution*, p.108.

NOTES AND REFERENCES

8   'Abdu'l-Bahá, *Promulgation*, p.5.
9   The Universal House of Justice, 'Promise,' *Messages*, p.685.
10 'Abdu'l-Bahá, *Promulgation*, p.305.
11 'Abdu'l-Bahá, *Promulgation*, p.38.
12 'Abdu'l-Bahá, *Promulgation*, pp. 38, 131.
13 Bahá'í International Community, 'Prosperity,' *Bahá'í World 1994-95*, p.288.
14 *Century of Light*, pp.108-9. The Universal House of Justice writes: 'The essential merit of spiritual principle is that it not only presents a perspective which harmonizes with that which is immanent in human nature, it also induces an attitude, a dynamic, a will, an aspiration, which facilitate the discovery and implementation of practical measures' (The Universal House of Justice, 'Promise,' *Messages*, p.690).
15 Esteva, 'Development,' *Development Dictionary*, p.8.
16 *Century of Light*, p.110.
17 'Abdu'l-Bahá, *Selections*, p.114.
18 'Abdu'l-Bahá, *Promulgation*, pp.97, 375.
19 'Abdu'l-Bahá, *Promulgation*, p.439.
20 'Abdu'l-Bahá, *Promulgation*, p.439.
21 The Universal House of Justice, 'Promise,' *Messages*, p.685.
22 Bahá'í International Community, 'Who Is Writing the Future?,' *Bahá'í World 1998-99*, p.261.
23 Armstrong, *History of God*, p.391.
24 Farzam Arbab, 'The Process of Social Transformation,' *The Bahá'í Faith and Marxism*, p.10.
25 Arbab, 'Process of Social Transformation,' *Bahá'í Faith and Marxism*, p.11.
26 Arbab, 'Process of Social Transformation,' *Bahá'í Faith and Marxism*, p.11.
27 Bahá'í International Community, 'Prosperity,' *Bahá'í World 1994-95*, p.276.
28 Armstrong, *History of God*, p.399.
29 Bahá'u'lláh, *Gleanings*, p.217.

A Spiritual Concept of Success

1 Anderson, *Reality*, pp.196-7.
2 Khavari, *Spiritual Intelligence*, p.243.
3 'Abdu'l-Bahá, *Promulgation*, p.303; *Paris Talks*, p.113; Bahá'u'lláh, 'Tarázát,' *Tablets*, p.35.
4 '[T]he view that there are not universal or objective ethical standards; that each culture develops the ethical standards that it finds acceptable and that these cannot be judged by the ethical standards of another culture' (*Oxford*, s.v. 'Relativism,' vol. 13, p.552).
5 The Parliament of the World's Religions, *A Global Ethic: The Declaration of the Parliament of the World's Religions*.
6 This commitment also implies that 'no humans have the right to use their

possessions without concern for the needs of society' (The Parliament of the World's Religions, *A Global Ethic*).
7 Levi, *Dialoghi*, p.11.
8 Matthew 16:16.
9 John 14:6.
10 Bhagavadgita XII, 18-20, *The Bhagavadgita*, pp.298-9.
11 Deuteronomy 6:5, 6.
12 John 14:15.
13 Bahá'u'lláh, 'Asl-i-Kullu'l-Khayr,' *Tablets*, p.155
14 Bahá'u'lláh, *Kitáb-i-Aqdas*, p.20.
15 Sarvepalli Radhakrishnan, 'Introductory Essay,' *The Bhagavadgita*, p.53.
16 Bahá'u'lláh, *Seven Valleys*, p.5.
17 Part of the concepts explained in this section are explained in greater details in Julio Savi, 'The Love relationship between God and Humanity: reflections on Bahá'u'lláh's *Hidden Words*,' *Bahá'í Studies Volume III. Scripture and Revelation*. Edited by Moojan Momen (Oxford: George Ronald, 1997), pp.283-307.
18 Cf. Matthew 5 and Luke 6:17-49.
19 Shoghi Effendi, *God Passes By*, p.140.
20 George Townshend, 'The "Hidden Words" of Bahá'u'lláh. A Reflection,' in *The Bahá'í World*, vol. 3, p.274.
21 Bahá'u'lláh, *The Hidden Words*, Persian, nos. 39, 41, 40, Arabic, no. 63, Persian, no. 58, Arabic, nos. 8, 40, 50, 68, Persian, no. 17.
22 Bahá'u'lláh, *Hidden Words*, Arabic, no.38. 'Abdu'l-Bahá considered love so important in view of spirituality that, in one of his speeches, he defined the latter as 'love in action' ('Abdu'l-Bahá, quoted in 'Join the Army of Peace,' *Star of the West*, vol. 13.5 (August, 1922), p.112).
23 Bahá'u'lláh, *Hidden Words*, Persian, nos. 43, 81, 82, 5.
24 Bahá'u'lláh, *Hidden Words*, Persian, no. 35, Arabic, no. 7.
25 Bahá'u'lláh writes: 'My first counsel is this: Possess a pure, kindly and radiant heart, that thine may be a sovereignty ancient, imperishable and everlasting' (Bahá'u'lláh, *Hidden Words*, Arabic, no. 1).
26 Bahá'u'lláh, *Hidden Words*, Persian, no. 58.
27 'Abdu'l-Bahá, *Promulgation*, p.129.
28 'Abdu'l-Bahá, *Promulgation*, p.49, *Some Answered Questions*, p.188.
29 'Constitution of the United Nations Educational Scientific and Cultural Organization,' United Nations Educational Scientific and Cultural Organization, *Basic Texts*, p.7.
30 Bahá'í International Community, 'Who Is Writing the Future?,' *Bahá'í World 1998-99*, p.266.
31 Bahá'í International Community, 'Who Is Writing the Future?,' *Bahá'í World 1998-99*, pp.265-6.
32 'Abdu'l-Bahá, *Paris Talks*, p.41, *Selections*, pp.287, 288.

33 'Abdu'l-Bahá, *Selections*, pp.256, 215.
34 Matthew 8:22.
35 Bahá'u'lláh, *Seven Valleys*, pp.4, 5.
36 Plato, *Alcibiades*, par. 29.
37 Khavari, *Spiritual Intelligence*, p.245.
38 Matthew 10:29-31.
39 Koran 9:51.
40 Bhagavadgita 3:9, *The Bhagavadgita*, p.135.
41 Sbert, 'Progress,' *Development Dictionary*, p.200.

A Spiritual Concept of Prosperity

1 Bahá'í International Community, 'Prosperity,' *Bahá'í World 1994-95*, p.288.
2 'Abdu'l-Bahá, *The Secret of Divine Civilization*, pp.61-3.
3 Giddens, *Modernity*, p.230.
4 *Webster*, s.v. 'Prosperity,' p.1821.
5 Cf. Loni Bramson-Lerche, 'An Analysis of the Bahá'í World Order Model,' *Emergence*, p.12.
6 Hossain B. Danesh, *Unity. The Creative Foundation of Peace*, p.118.
7 Yasna 30:10, *The Hymns of Zarathustra*, p.107.
8 Isaiah 2:4.
9 Koran 56:12, 25-6.
10 Bahá'í International Community, 'Who Is Writing the Future?,' *Bahá'í World 1998-99*, p.262.
11 *Century of Light*, p.22.
12 The Universal House of Justice, 'Promise,' *Messages*, p.687.
13 Hatcher, 'Love, Power and Justice,' *Journal of Bahá'í Studies*, vol. 9.3 (September, 1999), p.20.
14 Bahá'í International Community, 'Who Is Writing the Future?,' *Bahá'í World 1998-99*, p.266.
15 Bahá'í International Community, 'Prosperity,' *Bahá'í World 1994-95*, p.276.
16 *Millennium Forum Declaration,* http// www.millenniumforum.org/html/papers/mfd26May.html.
17 Bahá'í International Community, 'Who Is Writing the Future?,' *Bahá'í World 1998-99*, pp.263-4.
18 Bahá'u'lláh, quoted in *Messages*, p.376.
19 'Abdu'l-Bahá, *Selections*, p.302.
20 Bahá'í International Community, 'Prosperity,' *Bahá'í World 1994-95*, p.274.
21 For example, Anderson describes among the five metatrends of the emerging postmodern civilization the recognition of 'the centrality of learning to the life of every individual every society, and to the species as a whole' (Anderson, *Reality*, p.258).
22 Bahá'í International Community, 'Prosperity,' *Bahá'í World 1994-95*, p.284.

23 'Taking Dogmatism Seriously,' *World Order*, vol. 31.1 (Fall 1999), pp.2, 3.
24 Bahá'í International Community, 'Prosperity,' *Bahá'í World 1994-95*, pp.285, 286.
25 'Abdu'l-Bahá, quoted in Wendell Phillips Dodge, 'Abdul-Baha's Arrival in America,' *Star of the West*, vol. 3.3 (28 April 1912), p.4.
26 The Universal House of Justice, 'Promise,' *Messages*, pp.685, 689.
27 'Abdu'l-Bahá, *Promulgation*, p.197.
28 Bahá'í International Community, 'Prosperity,' *Bahá'í World 1994-95*, p.281.
29 Bahá'í International Community, 'Prosperity,' *Bahá'í World 1994-95*, p.293.
30 'Abdu'l-Bahá, *Selections*, p.283.
31 Bahá'í International Community, 'Prosperity,' *Bahá'í World 1994-95*, p.283.
32 'Abdu'l-Bahá, quoted in 'Trustworthiness,' *The Compilation of Compilations*, vol. 2, p.342.
33 Bahá'í International Community, 'Prosperity,' *Bahá'í World 1994-95*, pp.292, 293.
34 'Abdu'l-Bahá, *Secret*, pp.39, 14.
35 'Abdu'l-Bahá, *Secret*, pp.16, 22.
36 *Century of Light*, p.41.
37 Bahá'í International Community, 'Prosperity,' *Bahá'í World 1994-95*, p.294.
38 Bahá'í International Community, 'Prosperity,' *Bahá'í World 1994-95*, p.293.
39 The *Millennium Forum Declaration,* http// www.millenniumforum.org/html/papers/mfd26May.html.

A Spiritual Concept of Happiness

1 Rhett Diessner, 'Differentiating Physical, Social and Spiritual Emotions,' *Applied Spirituality: An Interdisciplinary Approach to the Advancement of Scholarship and Culture*.
2 'Abdu'l-Bahá, quoted in Rabb, 'Divine Art,' *Star of the West*, 7.12 (16 October 1917), p.162.
3 'Abdu'l-Bahá, quoted in Rabb, 'Divine Art,' *Star of the West*, vol. 7.12 (16 October 1917), p.162.
4 Khavari, *Spiritual Intelligence*, p.95.
5 'Abdu'l-Bahá, *Divine Philosophy*, p.130.
6 'Abdu'l-Bahá, *Promulgation*, pp.53, 52.
7 'Abdu'l-Bahá, *Promulgation*, pp.204-5.
8 'Abdu'l-Bahá, *Promulgation*, p.53.
9 'Abdu'l-Bahá, *Paris Talks*, p.108.
10 *Webster*, s.v. 'Self-respect,' p.2061.
11 'Abdu'l-Bahá, quoted in 'A Fortune That Bestows Eternal Happiness,' *Star of the West*, vol. 13.4 (17 May 1922), p.103.
12 'Abdu'l-Bahá, quoted in 'Fortune,' *Star of the West*, vol. 13.4 (17 May 1922), p.103.

13 'Abdu'l-Bahá, quoted in Rabb, 'Divine Art,' *Star of the West*, vol. 7.12 (16 October 1917), p.187.
14 Stephen R. Covey, *The Seven Habits of Highly-Effective People*, p.71.
15 'Abdu'l-Bahá, quoted in 'Fortune,' *Star of the West*, vol. 13.4 (17 May 1922), p.103.
16 Bahá'u'lláh, *Hidden Words*, Arabic, nos. 3, 4.
17 'Abdu'l-Bahá, *Selections,* p.27.
18 'Abdu'l-Bahá, *Secret*, pp.60, 46; *Promulgation*, p.372.
19 'Abdu'l-Bahá, quoted in Julia m: Grundy, *Ten Days in the Light of 'Akká*, p.39.
20 'Abdu'l-Bahá, quoted in Rabb, 'Divine Art,' *Star of the West*, vol. 7.12 (16 October 1917), p.161.
21 Bahá'u'lláh, *Hidden Words*, Arabic, no. 48.
22 Armstrong, *History of God*, p.378.
23 Battaglia, *Grande Dizionario*, s.v. 'Carattere,' vol. 2, p.740.
24 *Oxford*, s.v. 'Character,' vol. 3, p.31.
25 *Webster*, s.v. 'Character,' p.376.
26 *Dizionario di Psicologia*, s.v. 'Carattere,' pp.175, 176.
27 'Abdu'l-Bahá, *Promulgation*, p.427; *Secret*, pp.23, 60.
28 Bahá'u'lláh, 'Tarázát,' *Tablets*, p.36; quoted in 'Trustworthiness,' *Compilation*, vol. 2, p.332; *Gleanings*, p.272.
29 Xenophon, *Memorabilia*, ch. 1, par. 5.
30 'Abdu'l-Bahá, *Secret*, pp.55, 98, 40.
31 In the Bahá'í Scriptures the character is qualified as 'acceptable in His sight' (Bahá'u'lláh, *Gleanings*, p.272), 'fair' ('Abdu'l-Bahá, quoted in 'Trustworthiness,' *Compilation*, vol. 2, p.344), 'good', (Bahá'u'lláh, 'Tarázát,' *Tablets*, p.36), 'goodly' (Bahá'u'lláh, 'Lawh-i-Maqsúd,' *Tablets*, p.172), 'noble' (Bahá'u'lláh, quoted in 'Trustworthiness,' *Compilation*, vol. 2, p.331), 'praiseworthy' (Bahá'u'lláh, 'Kalimát-i-Firdawsíyyih,' *Tablets*, p.68), 'righteous' (Bahá'u'lláh, quoted in 'Trustworthiness,' *Compilation*, vol. 2, p.333), 'saintly' (Bahá'u'lláh, 'Lawh-i-Dunyá,' *Tablets*, p.88), 'shining and resplendent' (Bahá'u'lláh, 'Kitáb-i-'Ahd,' *Tablets*, p.220), 'spiritual' ('Abdu'l-Bahá, *Selections*, p.232), 'upright' (Bahá'u'lláh, 'Ishráqát,' *Tablets*, p.126), 'virtuous' (Bahá'u'lláh, *Epistle to the Son of the Wolf*, p.29) , but also as 'evil and unsound'('Abdu'l-Bahá, *Selections*, p.136).
32 'Abdu'l-Bahá, quoted in 'Bahá'í Education,' *Compilation*, vol. 1, pp. 282-3; *Selections*, p.136.
33 'Abdu'l-Bahá, *Secret*, p.54, Bahá'u'lláh, 'Ishráqát,' *Tablets*, p.121.
34 'Abdu'l-Bahá, *Promulgation*, p.166.
35 Khavari, *Spiritual Intelligence*, p.245.

A Conclusion
1 *Millennium Forum Declaration*, http// www.millenniumforum.org/html/papers/mfd26May.html.
2 Anderson, *Reality*, p.251-2.

Bibliography

'ABDU'L-BAHÁ, *'Abdu'l-Bahá on Divine Philosophy*. Boston, MA: The Tudor Press, 1918.
—'A Fortune that Bestows Eternal Happiness. Knowledge, Purity of Thought and Love. Talks given by 'Abdu'l-Bahá on Mount Carmel to a group of college students during their summer vacation,' *Star of the West*, vol. 13.4 (17 May 1922), pp.102-4.
—*Paris Talks: Addresses Given by 'Abdu'l-Bahá in Paris in 1911-1912*. 11th ed. London: Bahá'í Publishing Trust, 1969.
—*The Promulgation of Universal Peace. Talks delivered by 'Abdu'l-Bahá during His visit to the United States and Canada in 1912*. Compiled by Howard MacNutt, 2nd ed. Wilmette, IL: Bahá'í Publishing Trust, 1982.
—*The Secret of Divine Civilization*. Translated from the original Persian text by Marzieh Gail. Wilmette, IL: Bahá'í Publishing Trust, 1957.
—*Selections from the Writings of 'Abdu'l-Bahá*. Compiled by the Research Department of the Universal House of Justice and translated by a Committee at the Bahá'í World Centre and by Marzieh Gail. Haifa: Bahá'í World Centre, 1978.
—*Some Answered Questions*. Collected and translated from the Persian by Laura Clifford-Barney. 3rd ed. Wilmette, IL: Bahá'í Publishing Trust, 1981.
—'Tablet to Dr. Auguste Henri Forel,' *The Bahá'í World*, vol. 15, pp.37-43.
—*Tablets of 'Abdu'l-Bahá Abbas*. Vol. 2. 2nd ed. Chicago, IL: Bahá'í Publishing Society, 1919.

ANDERSON, Walter Truett. *Reality Isn't What It used To Be. Theatrical Politics, Ready To-Wear Religion, Global Myths, Primitive Chic, and Other Wonders of the Postmodern World*. San Francisco, CA: Harper Collins, 1990.

ANGELA, Piero. 'Le frontiere della scienza e delle tecnologia,' *Verso il duemila*, pp.141-69.

ANNAN, Kofi. 'Secretary-General Pledges "Quiet Revolution" in United Nations, Presents Reform Proposals to General Assembly,' United Nations Press Release SG/SM/6284/Rev.2 GA/9282/Rev.2, 16 July 1997.

BIBLIOGRAPHY

—'War: Foe of Development,' United Nations Press Release SG/SM/7187, 19 October 1999.

ARBAB, Farzam. 'The Process of Social Transformation,' *The Bahá'í Faith and Marxism*, pp.9-20.

ARMSTRONG, Karen. *A History of God. The 4,000-Year Quest of Judaism, Christianity and Islám*. New York, NY: Ballantine Books, 1994.

ARNOLD, Wilhelm. s.v. 'Carattere,' *Dizionario di Psicologia*, pp.175-6.

AUGUSTINE. ST., *On the Psalms*. Volume I, Psalms 1-29. Translated and Annotated by Dame Scholastica Hebgin and Dame Felicitas Corrigan Benedectines of Stanbrook England. Mahwah, NJ: Paulist Press, 1960.

Bahá'í Canada. A monthly news journal published by the National Spiritual Assembly of the Bahá'ís of Canada. Thornhill, Ontario.

The Bahá'í Faith and Marxism. Proceedings of a Conference Held January 1986. Ottawa, Canada: Bahá'í Studies Publications, 1987.

THE BAHÁ'Í INTERNATIONAL COMMUNITY. 'The Prosperity of Humankind,' *The Bahá'í World 1994-95*, p.273-96.
—'Who is Writing the Future? Reflections on the Twentieth Century,' *The Bahá'í World 1998-99*, pp.255-68.

The Bahá'í Studies Review. A publication of the Association for Bahá'í Studies for English-speaking Europe. London, United Kingdom.

'The Bahá'í Studies Seminar on Ethics and Methodology Held in Cambridge on 30 September and 1 October 1978. Comments by the Research Department at the World Centre,' The Universal House of Justice, *Messages from the Universal House of Justice 1963-1986. The Third Epoch of the Formative Age*, p.388-92.

The Bahá'í World. A Biennial International Record. Prepared under the supervision of the National Spiritual Assembly of the United States and Canada with the approval of Shoghi Effendi. Vol. 3. New York, NY: Bahá'í Publishing Committee, 1930.

The Bahá'í World. An International Record. Prepared under the supervision of The Universal House of Justice. Vol. 15. Haifa: Bahá'í World Centre, 1976.

The Bahá'í World 1994-5. An International Record. Haifa: Bahá'í World Centre, 1996.

The Bahá'í World 1996-97. An International Record. Haifa: Bahá'í World Centre, 1998.

The Bahá'í World 1998-99. An International Record. Haifa: Bahá'í World Centre, 2000.

BAHÁ'U'LLÁH. *Epistle to the Son of the Wolf.* Translated by Shoghi Effendi. Wilmette, IL: Bahá'í Publishing Trust, 1953.
—*Gleanings from the Writings of Bahá'u'lláh*. Translated by Shoghi Effendi. Rev. ed. Wilmette, IL: Bahá'í Publishing Committee, 1941.
—*The Hidden Words of Bahá'u'lláh*. Translated by Shoghi Effendi with the assistance of some English friends. Wilmette, IL: Bahá'í Publishing Trust, 1975.
—*The Kitáb-i-Aqdas. The Most Holy Book of Bahá'u'lláh*. Haifa: Bahá'í World Centre, 1992.
—*Kitáb-i-Íqán. The Book of Certitude*. Revealed by Bahá'u'lláh. Translated by Shoghi Effendi. 2nd ed. Wilmette, IL: Bahá'í Publishing Trust, 1970.
—*The Seven Valleys and the Four Valleys*. Translated by Marzieh Gail in consultation with Ali-Kuli K͟hán. 4th rev. ed. Wilmette, IL: Bahá'í Publishing Trust, 1991.
—*Tablets of Bahá'u'lláh Revealed after the Kitáb-i-Aqdas*. Compiled by the Research Department of the Universal House of Justice and translated by Habib Taherzadeh with the assistance of a Committee at the Bahá'í World Centre. Haifa: Bahá'í World Centre, 1978.

BATTAGLIA, Salvatore. *Grande Dizionario della Lingua Italiana*. Turin: Unione Tipografico-Editrice Torinese, vol. 2, 1962; vol. 5, 1968; vol. 10, 1978; vol. 14, 1988.

BAUSANI, Alessandro. *Saggi sulla Fede Bahá'í*. Rome: Casa Editrice Bahá'í, 1991.
—'Some Aspects of the Bahá'í Expressive Style,' *World Order*, vol. 2 (Winter 1978-79), pp.36-43.

BERTHOUD, Gérald. 'Market,' *Development Dictionary*, pp.70-87.

The Bhagavadgita, With an Introductory Essay, Sanskrit Text, English Translation and Notes by Sarvepalli Radhakrishnan. New Delhi: Indus, Harper Collins Publishers, 1993.

BRAMSON-LERCHE, Loni. 'An Analysis of the Bahá'í World Order Model,' *Emergence*, pp.1-70.

The Compilation of Compilations. Prepared by The Universal House of Justice 1963-1990. 2 vols. Maryborough, Victoria, Australia: Bahá'í Publications Australia, 1991.

Century of Light. Haifa: Bahá'í World Centre, 2001.

COMTE, Auguste. *The Positive Philosophy of Auguste Comte*. Translated by Harriet Martineau. Chicago New York [etc.]: Belford, Clarke & co. [188-].

'Constitution of the United Nations Educational Scientific and Cultural Organization Adopted in London on 16 November 1945 and amended by the General Conference at its 2nd, 3rd, 4th, 5th, 6th, 7th, 8th, 9th, 10th, 12th, 15th, 17th, 19th, 20th, 21st, 24th, 25th, 26th, 27th, 28th and 29th sessions,' United Nations Educational Scientific and Cultural Organization. *Basic Texts. 2000 edition including texts and amendments adopted by the General Conference at its 30th session*, pp. 5ff.

COVEY, Stephen R. *The Seven Habits of Highly-Effective People*. New York, NY: Fireside, 1989.

DANESH, Hossain B. *Unity. The Creative Foundation of Peace*. Rev. ed. Ottawa, Canada: Bahá'í Studies Publications, and Toronto, Canada: Fitzhenry-Whiteside, 1986.

De Darwin au darwinisme: science et idéologie. An International Congress for the Centenary of Darwin's Passing, Paris-Chantilly, 13-16 September 1982. Paris, 1983.

The Development Dictionary. A Guide to Knowledge as Power. Edited by Wolfgang Sachs. Johannesburg: Witwatersrand University Press, 1999.

DEVOTO, Giacomo and Gian Carlo OLI. *Dizionario della Lingua Italiana*. Florence: Le Monnier, 1971.

DIESSNER, Rhett. 'Differentiating Physical, Social and Spiritual Emotions.' Unpublished.

Dizionario analogico della lingua italiana. Turin: UTET - TEA, 1991.

Dizionario di Psicologia. Edited by Wilhelm Arnold, Hans Jurgen Eysenck, Richrad

Meili. Translated from the German by A. Messori, L. Pusci, M. De Nunzio, C. Danna and L. Giovannini. Edited by L. Giovannini, L. Pusci, E. Sgarbossa, A. Tergolina. 3rd ed. Cinisello Balsamo, Milan: Edizioni Paoline, 1986.

Documents on American Foreign Relations. Connecticut: Princeton University Press, 1967.

Emergence. Dimensions of a New World Order. Edited by Charles Lerche. London: Bahá'í Publishing Trust, 1991.

ESTEVA, Gustavo. 'Development,' *Development Dictionary*, pp.6-25.

GIAMMANCO, Roberto. *Dialogo sulla società americana.* Scandicci (Florence): La Nuova Italia, 1995.

GIDDENS, Anthony. *The Consequences of Modernity.* Stanford, CA: Stanford University Press, 1990.
—*Modernity and Self-Identity. Self and Society in the Late Modern Age.* Stanford, CA: Stanford University Press, 1991.

GRUNDY, Julia M. *Ten Days in the Light of 'Akká.* Rev. ed. Wilmette, IL: Bahá'í Publishing Trust, 1979.

HAECKEL, Ernst Heinrich. *The History of Creation of the Development of the Earth and its Inhabitants by the Action of Natural Causes.* 4th ed. London: K. Paul, Trench, Trübner & co., ltd., 1906.

HATCHER, William S. 'Love, Power and Justice,' *The Journal of Bahá'í Studies*, vol. 9.3, pp.1-23.

HEGEL, Georg Wilhelm Friedrich. *Lectures on the Philosophy of History by G.W.F. Hegel.* Translated from the 3d German ed. by J. Sibree. London: H.G. Bohn, 1861.

HOBSBAWM, Eric. *Age of Extremes. The Short Twentieth Century 1914-1991.* London: Abacus, 1995.

HOLMES, Oliver Wendell. *Ralph Waldo Emerson.* Boston, MA: Mifflin and co., 1885.

HUDDLESTON, John. 'Another Look at Achieving Peace by the Year 2000,' *The Journal of Bahá'í Studies*, vol. 9.2, pp.47-69.

BIBLIOGRAPHY

The Hymns of Zarathustra. Being a translation of the Gathas together with introduction and commentary by Jacques Duchesne-Guillemin. Translated from the French by Mrs. M. Henning. Boston, MA: Charles E. Tuttle Company, c. 1992.

'Issues Related to the Study of the Bahá'í Faith,' *Bahá'í Canada*, May 1998.

JAMES, William. *Pragmatism, a new name for some old ways of thinking.* New York, NY: Longman Green and Co, 1907.

The Journal of Bahá'í Studies. A publication of the Association for Bahá'í Studies. Ottawa.

KHAVARI, Khalil A. *Spiritual Intelligence. A Practical Guide to Personal Happiness.* New Liskeard, Ontario: White Mountains Publications, 2000.

KUHN, Thomas S. *The Structure of Scientific Revolution.* 2nd rev. ed. Chicago, IL: University of Chicago Press, 1970.

LASZLO, Ervin. *Evolution. The General Theory.* Cresskill, NJ: Hampton Press, 1996.

LEGRENZI, Paolo. *La felicità.* Bologna: Il Mulino, 1998.

LEVI, Arrigo. *Dialoghi sulla fede con Vincenzo Paglia e Andrea Riccardi.* Bologna: Il Mulino, 2000.

Lights of Guidance. A Bahá'í Reference File Compiled by Helen Basset Hornby. Rev. ed. New Delhi: Bahá'í Publishing Trust, 1996.

MARX, Karl. *Das Kapital. Buch 1: Der Productionprocess des Kapitals.* Hamburg: Meissner, 1867.

MELOGRANI, Piero. *La modernità e i suoi nemici.* Milan: Mondadori, 2000.

'Millennium Forum Declaration and Agenda for Action. Strengthening the United Nations for the 21st Century,' http://www.millenniumforum.org/html/papers/mfd26May.htm.

MINOIS, Georges. *Storia dell'ateismo.* Translated into Italian by Oreste Trabucco and Lelio La Porta. Rome: Editori Riuniti, 2000.

MONOD, Jacques. *Chance and Necessity. An Essay on the Natural Philosophy of Modern Biology.* Translated from the French by Austryn Wainhouse. London: Penguin Books, 1997.

MURCHIE, Guy. *The Seven Mysteries of Life. An Exploration in Science and Philosophy.* Boston, MA: Houghton Mifflin Company, 1978.

NATOLI, Salvatore. *La felicità. Saggio di teoria degli affetti.* 5th ed. Milan: Feltrinelli, 1998.

The Oxford Dictionary of World Religions. Edited by John Bowker. Oxford: Oxford University Press, 1997.

The Oxford English Dictionary. Second Edition Prepared by J.A. Simpson and E.S.C. Weiner. Oxford: Clarendon Press, 1989.

PARLIAMENT OF THE WORLD'S RELIGIONS. *A Global Ethic: The Declaration of the Parliament of the World's Religions.* Edited by Hans Küng and Karl-Josef Kuschel. New York, NY: Continuum, 1993.

PHILLIPS DODGE, Wendell. 'Abdu'l-Bahá's Arrival in America,' *Star of the West*, vol. 3. 3, pp.3-6.

PLATO, *Alcibiades*, translated by Sanderson Beck. http://www.san.beck.org/Alcibiades2.html.

PROVINE, William B. 'Mécanisme, dessein et éthique: la révolution darwinienne inachevée,' *De Darwin au darwinisme: science et idéologie*, pp.119.

RABB, Mary M. 'The Divine Art of Living. A Compilation by Mrs. Mary M. Rabb,' *Star of the West*, vol. 7.16 (31 December 1916), pp.149-55, 161-4; vol. 7.18 (7 February 1917), pp.177-88; vol. 7.19 (2 March 1917), pp.195-6; vol. 8.2 (9 April 1917), pp.17-21, 23-8; vol. 8.4 (17 May 1917), pp.41-8; vol. 8.6 (24 June 1917), pp.57-61, 63-8; vol. 8.8 (1 August 1917), pp.85-8, 96-104; vol. 8.10 (8 September 1917), pp.121-7, 134-6; vol. 8.11 (27 September 1917), pp.137-44; vol. 8.18 (7 February 1918), pp.229-36; vol. 8.19 (2 March 1918), pp.238-44.

RADHAKRISHNAN, Sarvepalli. 'Introductory Essay,' *The Bhagavadgita*, pp. 11-78.

RUSSEL, Bertrand. *The Scientific Outlook.* Glencoe, IL: The Free Press, 1931.

BIBLIOGRAPHY

SACHS, Wolfgang. 'Introduction,' *Development Dictionary*, pp.1-5.

SAVATER, Fernando. *Le domande della vita*. Translated into Italian by Francesca Saltarelli. Bari: Laterza, 1999.

SBERT, José María. 'Progress,' *Development Dictionary*, pp.192-205.

SCHIMMEL, Annemarie. *Mystical Dimensions of Islam*. Chapel Hill, NC: The University of North Carolina Press, 1975.

SHOGHI EFFENDI. *God Passes By*. Introduction by George Townshend. Wilmette, IL: Bahá'í Publishing Trust, 1957.

SOROKIN. Pitirim A. *The Crisis of Our Age*. 2nd rev. ed. Oxford: Oneworld, 1992.

Star of the West. A Bahá'í periodical published from 1910 to 1933 in Chicago and Washington D.C.

'Taking Dogmatism Seriously. Editorial,' *World Order*, vol. 31.1 (Fall 1999), pp.2-3.

TOWNSHEND, George. 'The "Hidden Words" of Bahá'u'lláh. A Reflection,' *The Bahá'í World*, vol. 3, pp.274-7.

TRUMAN, Harry S. 'Inaugural Address, January 20, 1949,' *Documents on American Foreign Relations*.

UNITED NATIONS EDUCATIONAL SCIENTIFIC AND CULTURAL ORGANIZATION. *Basic Texts. 2000 edition including texts and amendments adopted by the General Conference at its 30th session*. Paris: UNESCO, 2000.

THE UNIVERSAL HOUSE OF JUSTICE. *Messages from the Universal House of Justice 1963-1986: The Third Epoch of the Formative Age*. Compiled by Geoffry W. Marks. Wilmette, IL: Bahá'í Publishing Trust, 1996.
— 'The Promise of World Peace. Text of a Statement Issued by the Universal House of Justice,' *Messages from the Universal House of Justice 1963-1986*, pp.681-96.

Verso il duemila. Various authors. Bari: Laterza, 1984.

Webster's Third New International Dictionary of the English Language Unabridged.

Utilizing all the experience and resources of more than one hundred years of Merriam-Webster dictionaries. Editor in chief Philip Babcock Gove, Ph.D. and the Merriam-Webster Editorial Staff. 3rd ed. Springfield, MA: Merriam-Webster Inc., 1986.

WEINBERG, Matthew. 'The Human Rights Discourse. A Bahá'í Perspective,' in *The Bahá'í World 1996-97*, pp.247-73.

World Order. A Bahá'í quarterly published by the National Spiritual Assembly of the Bahá'ís of the United States. Wilmette, IL, USA.

XENOPHON. *The Memorabilia or Recollections of Socrates.* Translated by Henry Graham Dakyns. London: Macmillan and Co., [c.1895].